MOZZARELLA

First published in 1999 by Periplus Editions (HK) Ltd., with editorial offices
at 153 Milk Street, Boston, Massachusetts 02109.

Created by Co & Bear Productions (UK) Ltd.
Copyright © 1998 Co & Bear Productions Ltd.
Photographs copyright © 1998 Sian Irvine.

Library of Congress Cataloging-in-Publication Data

Mozzarella : inventive recipes from leading chefs with buffalo
mozzarella / photographed by Sian Irvine.
    p. cm.
  Includes index.
  ISBN 962-593-439-1 (hc)
  1. Cookery (Mozzarella cheese) 2. Mozzarella cheese. 3. Cookery,
Italian. I. Irvine, Sian.
  TX759 . 5 . C48 M69 1999
  641.6'73—dc21

                                    98—41791
                                       CIP

Distributed by

USA
Charles E. Tuttle Co., Inc.
RR 1 Box 231-5
North Clarendon, VT
05759
Tel: (802) 773-8930
Tel: (800) 526-2778

CANADA
Raincoast Books
8680 Cambie Street
Vancouver, V6P 6M9
Tel: (604) 323-7100
Fax: (604) 323-2600

JAPAN
Tuttle Shokai Ltd.
1-21-13, Seki
Tama-ku, Kawasaki-shi
Kanagawa-ken 214, Japan
Tel: (044) 833-0225
Fax: (044) 822-0413

SOUTHEAST ASIA
Berkeley Books Pte. Ltd.
5 Little Road #08-01
Singapore 536983
Tel: (65) 280-3320
Fax: (65) 280-6290

1 3 5 7 9 10 8 6 4 2
05 04 03 02 01 00 99

Printed and bound in Novara, Italy by Officine Grafiche de Agostini

INVENTIVE RECIPES
FROM LEADING CHEFS
WITH BUFFALO MOZZARELLA

MOZZARELLA

PHOTOGRAPHED BY
SIAN IRVINE

PERIPLUS

Contents

The Art of Making Buffalo Mozzarella

Above: *Buffaloes arrived in the south of Italy from India in the sixteenth century, and locals quickly saw the advantages of making cheese with the rich, flavorsome milk.*

In the terraced houses that line the winding streets of Naples, and in the farm kitchens of the rugged southern Italian countryside of Campania with its fertile volcanic soil, mozzarella has long been a staple part of the local diet. No one knows exactly how long the cheese has been made in the south of Italy, but as early as A.D. 60 the Romans are recorded as making a similar food, curdling fresh milk with rennet extracted from the stomach of a sheep or goat.

Legend also has it that the monks of San Lorenzo di Capua gave bread and "mozza" cheese to the hungry who came knocking on the convent door in the third century. Eventually, the soft mozza cheese reputedly made by the monks became known as "mozzarella." The word derives from the Italian verb *mozzare*, to cut off, the action of breaking the cheese curd into smaller, more manageable portions.

The transition of mozzarella made from sheep's milk to what is now considered the real thing—made from the creamy milk of buffaloes—came many centuries after the monks of San Lorenzo earned a reputation for their cheese.

Indian water buffaloes, which roam wild in southeastern Asia, were first introduced to Campania and other areas of southern Italy in the sixteenth century. They thrived in the mild, dry climate, producing a rich,

flavorsome milk from which the cheese makers in the provincial capital, Naples, made buffalo mozzarella, or *mozzarella di bufala* as it is known locally.

Along with the region's passion for spaghetti, and its delicious plum tomatoes, considered the best in Italy, buffalo mozzarella became synonymous with Naples.

Over the centuries, the Neapolitans earned a reputation for their love of food and other sensuous pleasures. In the nineteenth century, when Naples became the fashionable heart of Italy, local dishes became popular all over the country. While those pursuing intellectual or artistic pursuits could revel in the antiquities of nearby Pompei or Pozzuoli, matters of gastronomy were best satisfied in Naples itself.

A stroll around the narrow lanes and markets in those days would reveal a banquet of tasty meals and snacks: spaghetti stalls serving up steaming plates of pasta topped with a sauce of succulent plum tomatoes; stands hawking savory fritters and fresh seafood; the *gelatiere* scooping ice cream from his barrow; and, most famous of all, the baker plying slices of crisply baked dough topped with oil and herbs.

Pizza Napoli, as it has come to be called the world over, was baked in wood-fired ovens, initially only seasoned with a few drops of olive oil, a sprinkling of herbs, and perhaps salted anchovies. The dish had provided nourishment to generations of Neapolitans for at least two centuries before Italy's royal couple visited the regional capital in 1899, ordering pizza to show their solidarity with the people. According to local annals, the baker concerned wanted to add a little something extra in the couple's honor, so he garnished the pizza in the colors of Italy's flag: with slices of thick white buffalo

Above: *The best buffalo mozzarella is still made by hand, and is checked at each stage to ensure optimum taste.*

mozzarella, red tomatoes, and green basil leaves. He named it after the queen, Margherita, and the dish still bears her name.

Today, mozzarella is made in much the same way as it was when used on that first Pizza Margherita. Just as daylight is breaking over the gentle hills of Campania, the buffalo milk from the provincial farms is distributed among the small cheese makers dotting Naples and the surrounding countryside, who make fresh mozzarella from it daily.

The milk arrives just after dawn and is poured into large aluminium tanks, allowing 4½ quarts (4.5 liters) of milk for every 2 pounds (1kg) of the finished cheese. The milk is heated to 95°F (35°C) for three or four hours and then a few drops of concentrated fluid are added to coagulate the milk, a process that takes about twenty minutes. The coagulant, called *caglio*, is in fact extracted from the intestinal fluid of sheep when

they are slaughtered, and is used to set the cheese, just as it was in ancient Roman days.

Once the curd has formed it needs to be broken up into smaller pieces, with excess liquid cheese being drained away to form the delicious buffalo ricotta. The firm cheese that remains is heated until it achieves just the right elasticity.

After three hours the cheese maker selects a portion of the cheese and scoops it up with a wooden palette. If the cheese slides readily on the palette when hot water is poured over it, it is ready. If not, it goes back into the tank, to be tested again at five-minute intervals until it passes muster.

At this point the cheese is ready to be rolled into balls by hand, an art that is learned over years of apprenticeship, and then soaked in brine for several hours before the whole process is complete.

Above: *Once the milk has coagulated, excess liquid is drained away to form buffalo ricotta.*

Above: *The experienced hands of the Neapolitan cheese maker know exactly when the mozzarella has reached the perfect elasticity.*

Aficionados of buffalo mozzarella have their favorite makers, specifying a number of prerequisites that must be satisfied. The best cheese makers usually run a small operation, with the freshness and quality of the cheese their main consideration. They should have been around for at least three generations, the craft having been passed from grandfather to father to son.

The maker should also be located fairly close to the farm providing the buffalo milk, no further than half an hour's drive, as the milk does not travel well over long distances. Most significantly, only natural ingredients must be used. Some larger manufacturers treat the fresh milk in order to extend the shelf life from a few days to a few weeks, but the resulting cheese is rubbery and tasteless.

Naturally made buffalo mozzarella only lasts about four or five days, and so the makers must ensure their product is speedily dispatched to the stores, restaurants and distributors they supply. The individual skills of the shop floor staff also come into play in creating the perfect cheese, but in the end the choice of a favorite maker boils down to the taste of the final product.

Freshly rolled mozzarella is at its peak just eight to ten hours after production when it is at its most elastic. It is certainly best eaten within a day or two, still dripping with the delicate, flavorsome buffalo milk. The mound of cheese should be glazed white with the sheen of the buffalo milk, and when sliced open should immediately reveal a trail of whey. It should still smell of the fragrant, lactic fermentation of the milk.

Cow's milk mozzarella is still produced in Italy and elsewhere, but cannot compare to the rich, moist buffalo version, with its milky taste and soft, succulent texture. Devoured as is, with perhaps some slices of tomato, or a handful of olives, it provides one of the most delicious sensations of summer eating.

Francesco Moncada di Paternò

Above: *Fresh, hand-rolled buffalo mozzarella is best eaten within a day or two.*

Insalata

Dean Carr / THE AVENUE
Broiled Vegetable & Mozzarella Salad with Roast Garlic

Matthew Harris / BIBENDUM
Spiced Artichoke Salad

Lorenzo Berni / SAN LORENZO
Insalata del Principe di Napoli

John Torode / MEZZO
Roast Tomato Salad with Sorrel & Artichoke Hearts

Alberto Chiappa / MONTPELIANO
Insalata alla Sophia

Henrik Iversen / QUAGLINO'S
Warm Salad of Buffalo Mozzarella & Chanterelles with Cabernet Vinegar

Alberico Penati / HARRY'S BAR
Chilled Tomato & Bocconcini Salad

Nino Sassu / ASSAGGI
Eggplant Salad with Carta Musica

Broiled Vegetable & Mozzarella Salad with Roast Garlic

INGREDIENTS

serves 4

¼ cup (2floz/60ml)
   white wine

juice of 1 lemon

⅔ cup (5floz/160ml)
   olive oil

2 pinches thyme leaves

2 pinches rosemary leaves

2 cloves garlic, chopped

4 baby artichokes

12 cloves garlic, peeled

1 medium red bell pepper
   (capsicum)

1 sweet potato

1 large zucchini (courgette)

1 medium eggplant
   (aubergine)

2 balls (2oz/60g each)
   buffalo mozzarella

2 bunches arugula (rocket)

¼ cup (2floz/60ml)
   balsamic vinegar

ground pepper

METHOD

1 *Fill a small pan with water and add the white wine, lemon juice, a splash of the olive oil, 1 pinch of thyme, 1 pinch of rosemary and a clove of chopped garlic. Bring to a boil and leave to simmer.*

2 *Meanwhile, snap off all the stalks of the artichokes and use a sharp knife to trim around the leaves, discarding all the outer ones. Place in the pan for about 6–8 minutes. Remove the pan from the heat but leave the artichokes sitting in the cooking liquor.*

3 *Wrap the whole cloves of garlic in foil and place in a preheated 350°F (180°C) oven for 5–6 minutes, or until tender.*

4 *Broil (grill) the red pepper until charred on all sides, place in a bowl and cover with plastic wrap (cling film). Allow to cool. When cold, peel, seed and quarter. Set aside.*

5 *Slice the sweet potato, zucchini and eggplant into ¾-inch (2-cm) pieces; cut the artichokes in half. Place them under the broiler (grill). Once cooked, sprinkle with the remaining chopped garlic, and pinches of thyme and rosemary and some of the olive oil to marinate.*

6 *Slice each ball of mozzarella into 6 pieces.*

7 *To assemble the dish, arrange the grilled vegetables on a plate with the mozzarella and arugula leaves. Drizzle the remaining olive oil and balsamic vinegar over and around the dish and add the roasted garlic, finishing with a twist of freshly ground pepper over the mozzarella.*

Spiced Artichoke Salad

(recipe on following page)

Spiced Artichoke Salad

INGREDIENTS

serves 6

4 globe artichokes

juice of 3 lemons

½ cup (4floz/120ml) plus
about 2 tbsp olive oil

½ cup (4floz/120ml) white
wine

1 bay leaf

1 bunch thyme

9 cloves garlic, peeled

salt

6 tomatoes, peeled

2 onions, thinly sliced

2 tsp ground cumin

1 tsp ground allspice

1 tsp saffron strands

handful of dried currants

1 bunch cilantro (coriander)

1 bunch flat-leaf parsley

3 balls (4oz/125g each)
buffalo mozzarella

6 slices country-style bread

METHOD

1 *In advance trim the
artichokes of all their leaves
so you are left with just the
heart and choke.*

2 *Place the hearts and
chokes in a saucepan with
3 qt (3l) of water and the
lemon juice. Also add ½ cup
(4floz/125ml) each of olive
oil and white wine, the bay
leaf, thyme, 6 of the garlic
cloves and a pinch of salt.
Cook for about 20 minutes.
They are ready when a
pointed knife goes in easily.*

3 *When the artichokes are
ready, allow them to cool in
the liquor and refrigerate
until you are ready to make
the salad. Reserve some
of the liquor for later.*

4 *Before you start cooking
the salad, remove the chokes
from the cooked artichokes
and dice the hearts. Seed
tomatoes, dice and reserve.
Remove the leaves from the
parsley and cilantro and
chop; reserve.*

5 *To make the salad, take a
large frying pan, add about
1 tbsp of the olive oil and fry
the onions over medium
heat until just golden brown.
Then add the cumin, allspice
and the remaining 3 cloves
of garlic, chopped. While this
is gently frying, heat up
2 tbsp of the artichoke liquor
and add the saffron to
infuse. After a couple of
minutes add the liquor to the
frying onions.*

6 *Now add the diced
artichoke and currants and
stew for 3–5 minutes, adding
more olive oil or artichoke
cooking liquor if the ingredients start to stick.*

7 *Remove from heat, add
chopped parsley, cilantro and
tomato, and leave to cool.*

8 *Meanwhile slice the mozzarella balls and grill 6 slices
of country-style bread.*

9 *Serve a large spoonful
of the artichoke salad on
each plate, along with a
couple of slices of buffalo
mozzarella, a drizzle of
olive oil and some grilled
country-style bread.*

INGREDIENTS

serves 4

2 avocados

4 ripe tomatoes

4 buffalo mozzarella
  treccine, about 3½ oz
  (100g) each (or balls if
  treccine not available)

¼ cup (2floz/60ml)
  olive oil

salt & ground pepper

basil leaves

Insalata del Principe di Napoli

METHOD

1 *Cut the avocados in half, remove the pits, peel and slice.*

2 *Slice the tomatoes.*

3 *In the center of each plate, place 1 of the small mozzarella treccine. On one side arrange the tomato slices, and on the other the avocado slices.*

4 *Drizzle over the olive oil to taste, add salt and pepper, and garnish with some fresh basil leaves.*

Roast Tomato Salad with Sorrel & Artichoke Hearts

INGREDIENTS

Serves 4

4 large, ripe tomatoes

2 balls (4oz/125g each)
   buffalo mozzarella, sliced

leaves from 1 bunch flat-
   leaf parsley

2 shallots, sliced paper-thin

1 bunch sorrel, tough
   stems removed

2 marinated artichoke
   hearts, halved lengthwise

ground pepper

DRESSING

1 bunch sorrel, julienned

½ cup (4floz/125ml)
   olive oil

salt & ground pepper

METHOD

1 *Cut tomatoes into thick slices. Place on a baking sheet (tray) on parchment (grease-proof) paper. Sprinkle with salt, and place in the bottom of a preheated 300°F (150°C) oven and bake until dried.*

2 *Overlap tomatoes and mozzarella in a tight circle around each plate.*

3 *Mix dressing ingredients and use a small amount to toss with the parsley, shallots and sorrel.*

4 *Place parsley mixture on top of the tomatoes and mozzarella. Top each serving with an artichoke half.*

5 *Drizzle dressing on top, and season with pepper.*

Note: For a more refined alternative to the dressing, puree the sorrel, then add olive oil, to make sorrel oil. Season with salt and pepper.

INGREDIENTS

serves 4

1 head red oak-leaf lettuce or
  radicchio (red chicory), 4 oz
  (125ml)

1 head lolla rossa lettuce or
  other loose-leaf lettuce

1 head frisée

4 plum tomatoes, sliced

4 oz (125g) canned tuna,
  flaked (about ⅔ cup)

2 balls (4oz/125g each)
  buffalo mozzarella, diced

½ red bell pepper (capsicum)

½ yellow bell pepper (capsicum)

1 avocado

salt & pepper

2 tbsp white wine vinegar

4 eggs

¼ cup (2floz/60ml) olive oil

1 dried chilli pepper

1 clove garlic

½ baguette, cut into bite-
  sized croutons

DRESSING

2 tbsp balsamic vinegar

1 tsp brown sugar

1 green (spring) onion, minced

pinch of finely chopped
  fresh ginger

¼ cup (2floz/60ml) extra-
  virgin olive oil

Insalata alla Sophia

METHOD

1 Carefully wash and dry all the salad leaves, place them in a large bowl and add the tomatoes, tuna and mozzarella.

2 Chop the bell peppers, and peel, pit and chop the avocado; add them to the salad. Season with salt and pepper and set aside.

3 In a shallow pan, bring 4 cups (32floz/1l) water to a boil. Add the white wine vinegar and a pinch of salt. Break the eggs 1 at a time into a ladle and lower into the water to poach. Lift out and set aside the poached eggs.

4 In a frying pan, heat the olive oil and add the chili and garlic. Then add the croutons and fry until golden brown. Set aside.

5 For the dressing, mix together the balsamic vinegar with the brown sugar, green onion and ginger. Add the olive oil and mix again.

6 Season the salad with the dressing and divide among 4 plates, along with a sprinkling of croutons. When ready to serve, place a poached egg on top of each portion.

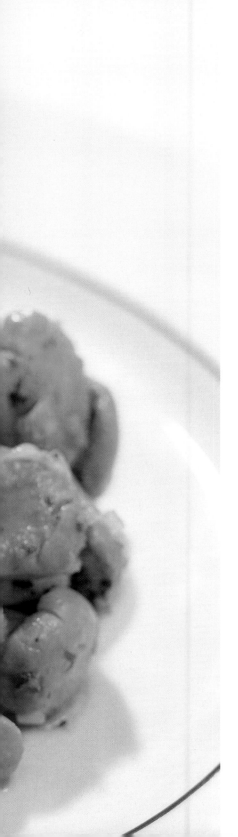

Warm Salad of Buffalo Mozzarella & Chanterelles with Cabernet Vinegar

METHOD

1 *In a hot frying pan, lightly color the shallot in a small amount of olive oil.*

2 *Add the mushrooms, season with salt and pepper and sauté for 2–3 minutes, or until just tender. Add the garlic and cook for a further 30 seconds.*

3 *Transfer the mushrooms to a bowl and add the mozzarella.*

4 *Return the pan to heat, pour in the cabernet vinegar, reduce by three-fourths, then pour over the mushrooms.*

5 *Add the chopped parsley, toss and divide the salad among 4 plates.*

INGREDIENTS

serves 4

1 large shallot, chopped

olive oil

9 oz (250g) fresh chanter-elle (girolle) mushrooms

salt & ground pepper

2 cloves garlic, sliced paper-thin

2 balls (4 oz/100g each) buffalo mozzarella, cut in half and sliced

3 tbsp cabernet vinegar or other red wine vinegar

⅓ cup (½ oz/15g) chopped parsley

INGREDIENTS

serves 4

1 package (1tbsp/¼oz/7g)
    powdered gelatin

12 oz (375g) ripe tomatoes,
    puréed and strained

salt & ground pepper

4 asparagus spears

4 baby fennel bulbs

16 mozzarella bocconcini

8 oz (250g) ripe tomatoes,
    cut into cubes

⅓ cup (3floz/80ml) extra-
    virgin olive oil

leaves from 1 bunch basil,
    finely chopped

chervil for garnish

Chilled Tomato & Bocconcini Salad

METHOD

1 Soak gelatin in ¼ cup (2floz/60ml) water for 3–5 minutes then stir to disolve.

2 Mix the strained tomato juice with a little salt and pepper and the dissolved gelatin, and refrigerate until set, about 30 minutes.

3 Boil the asparagus and the baby fennel in salted water until just tender. Drain and dress with half the oil and basil.

4 Remove the set tomato aspic from the refrigerator and chop roughly. Place a layer of the aspic in the bottom of 4 small dishes.

5 Trim the fennel and asparagus and stand several sections in the aspic, along with 4 bocconcini and the chopped tomatoes dressed with the remaining basil and oil. Garnish with chervil.

Eggplant Salad
& Carta Musica

METHOD

1 Cut tomatoes into thick slices. Place on a baking sheet (tray) on parchment (grease-proof) paper. Sprinkle with salt, and place in the bottom of a preheated 300°F (150°C) oven and bake until dried.

2 Cut the eggplant into thin slices. Sprinkle with salt and set aside for 20 minutes. Dry the slices with a paper towel and brush lightly with some of the olive oil. Place in a preheated 400°F (200°C) oven for 3–5 minutes, or until soft. Sprinkle with basil if desired.

3 Sauté the eggplant in a nonstick pan, without any extra oil, over high heat until golden brown on both sides. Remove to a plate and drizzle over a little of the olive oil and 1 tsp of the balsamic vinegar. Shave the garlic clove with a vegetable peeler, and place shavings atop the eggplant to infuse it. Add a little more basil, if desired.

4 Cut the mozzarella into slices. Arrange the radicchio and most of the arugula on the base of each plate. Place the bread on top of this, and then arrange slices of mozzarella, eggplant and tomato, alternating them to create a fan. Sprinkle with basil and the remainig arugula, olive oil and balsamic vinegar.

INGREDIENTS

serves 2

2 large, ripe tomatoes

salt

1 small eggplant
  (aubergine)

2 tbsp extra-virgin
  olive oil

handful of chopped basil

about 2 tsp balsamic
  vinegar

1 garlic clove

1 ball (8oz/250g)
  buffalo mozzarella

2 sheets Carta Musica
  flat bread (see page 154;
  soften by sprinkling with
  water and shaking off
  excess)

1 head radicchio (red
  chicory), separated
  into leaves

1 bunch arugula (rocket),
  tough stems removed

Pane

Michael Moore / BLUEBIRD
Flat Bread with Bocconcini, Spices & Anchovies

David Burke / LE PONT DE LA TOUR
Panfried Ciabatta Sandwich with Buffalo Mozzarella

Antonello Tagliabue / BICE
Focaccia Toscana with Mozzarella, Roasted Peppers & Basil Cream

John Torode / MEZZO
Brioche with Peppers, Eggplants & Mozzarella

Paul Wilson / GEORGES
Crescenta of Mozzarella & Roasted Peppers with Anchoiade

Sally Clarke / CLARKE'S
Baked Shallot & Oven-Dried Tomato Focaccia with Bocconcini

Michael Moore / BLUEBIRD
Rotolo of Wood-Roasted Eggplant & Peppers with Brioche

Alastair Little / ALASTAIR LITTLE
Focaccia with Buffalo Mozzarella & Rosemary

Michael Moore / BLUEBIRD
Polenta, Mozzarella & Prosciutto Sandwich

INGREDIENTS

serves 4

2 tsp active dry yeast

½ tsp sugar

1½ cups (12 fl oz/375ml)
   warm water

3½ cups (1 lb/500g) all-
   purpose (plain) flour

1 tsp baking soda (bicar-
   bonate of soda)

1 egg

¼ cup (2 fl oz/60ml) olive oil

olive oil for brushing

about 2 tbsp fennel seeds

sea salt

ground pepper

20 small black grapes

TOPPING

6–8 anchovy fillets

1 tbsp salted capers
   (rinsed)

½ bunch flat-leaf parsley

8 oz (250g) buffalo
   mozzarella bocconcini

extra-virgin olive oil

Flat Bread with Bocconcini, Spices & Anchovies

METHOD

1 Mix the yeast, sugar and warm water together in a small bowl. Let stand for 4 minutes.

2 Place the flour and baking soda together in a separate large bowl.

3 Beat the egg and add to the yeast mix, then combine with the flour using a stand mixer fitted with the paddle attachment on a slow speed.

4 Add the olive oil and continue to mix for another 3 minutes until smooth.

5 Cover the bowl with a damp kitchen towel and leave the dough to rise for 20 minutes.

6 Knead the dough briefly on a lightly floured surface until smooth and elastic, then separate into 4 equal balls. Shape each ball into a pizza base.

7 Preheat an oven to 450°F (230°C). Brush the pizza bases with olive oil, and sprinkle with fennel seeds, salt, pepper and grapes. Leave to rise for 10 minutes.

8 Bake in the hot oven for 8 minutes.

9 Meanwhile, for the topping, roughly chop together the anchovies, capers and parsley.

10 When the bread is cooked, slice the bocconcini onto it, sprinkle the parsley mixture over, drizzle with olive oil and serve.

Note: This dish may be served warm or cold. To warm, place in a 450°F (230°C) oven or under a preheated broiler (grill) for 2 minutes before dressing.

Panfried Ciabatta Sandwich with Buffalo Mozzarella

METHOD

1 *Place each slice of prosciutto on a slice of ciabatta so that it overhangs the bread.*

2 *Cut the mozzarella into 12 even slices and place 3 pieces on top of each prosciutto slice.*

3 *Fold the overhanging prosciutto up and over the mozzarella to form an envelope, and place the remaining slice of ciabatta on top, pressing down gently.*

4 *In a heavy-bottomed pan, heat the olive oil. When the oil is hot, dip each sandwich in egg on both sides and place in the pan. Cook evenly on both sides until golden brown, with the mozzarella slightly melting.*

5 *Serve immediately with a simple dressed salad.*

INGREDIENTS

Serves 4

4 thin slices prosciutto

1 loaf ciabatta or other
  country-style bread,
  cut into 8 sandwich-
  sized slices

2 balls (4oz/125g each)
  buffalo mozzarella

2 tbsp olive oil

4 eggs, beaten & seasoned
  with salt & ground pepper

INGREDIENTS

serves 4

FOCACCIA

4 cups (1¼ lb/600g) all-
   purpose (plain) flour

1 envelope (2½ tsp) active
   dry yeast

1 cup plus 2 tbsp (9floz/
   250ml) warm water

1 tbsp milk

¼ cup (2floz/50ml) olive oil

1 tbsp table salt

olive oil for brushing

rosemary leaves

coarse sea salt

BASIL SAUCE

3 tbsp chopped green (spring)
   onions

1 tbsp butter

1 small potato, about 2oz (60g),
   peeled and thinly sliced

1½ cups (1½oz/40g) basil
   leaves

1 cup plus 2 tbsp (9floz/
   250ml) vegetable stock

pinch of salt

TOPPING

2 red bell peppers (capsicum)

salt & ground pepper

2 balls (5oz/150g each) buffalo
   mozzarella, cut into 12 slices

mixed salad leaves

Focaccia Toscana with Mozzarella, Roasted Peppers & Basil Cream

METHOD

1 *Mound the flour on a work surface and form a well in the center. Dissolve the yeast in the warm water, then add the milk, the olive oil and the salt. Place the mixed liquid in the well and gradually work into the flour. Then knead until the dough is smooth and elastic. Form it into a smooth ball shape, cover with a kitchen towel and let it rise for 1 hour.*

2 *On a lightly floured surface, roll out the dough ¼ inch (6mm) thick. Cut out 4 equal rounds and place them on a large greased baking sheet (tray). Sprinkle with water, brush with olive oil and scatter some rosemary leaves and coarse sea salt on top of each. Bake in a preheated 425°F (220°C) oven for 8–10 minutes, or until golden, then allow to cool.*

3 *Meanwhile, for the sauce, sauté the green onions in a pan with the butter until golden. Add the potato, half of the basil, the stock and salt. Let cook for 15 minutes.*

4 *Transfer the mix to a blender, add the rosemary and basil and blend well. Reheat gently; keep warm.*

5 *For the topping, using a vegetable peeler, peel the bell peppers, remove the seeds and cut into slices. Place them on a baking sheet (tray), sprinkle with salt and pepper and place in a preheated 425°F (220°C) oven until caramelized.*

6 *Cut the prepared focaccia rounds in half horizontally and fill each with 3 slices of mozzarella, 2 spoonfuls of hot basil sauce and a few slices of red pepper. Decorate with the salad leaves.*

Note: Suggested salad leaves include radicchio (red chicory), arugula (rocket) and watercress.

Brioche with Peppers, Eggplants & Mozzarella

INGREDIENTS

serves 4 or 5

1 lb (500g) eggplants
(aubergines)

1 lb (500g) red bell
peppers (capsicum)

1 lb (500g) buffalo
mozzarella, sliced

5 oz (150g) mixed salad
leaves

⅔ cup (5floz/150ml) salad
dressing

½ cup (4floz/120ml) olive
oil

1 egg, beaten

METHOD

1 Preheat a broiler (grill). Cut the eggplants into slices ¼ inch (6mm) thick. Season with salt and pepper, brush with some of the olive oil and broil (grill) lightly.

2 Preheat the oven to 400°F (200°C). Brush the peppers with the remaining olive oil. Roast in the oven for around 20 minutes to blacken, then cool, peel off the skin and discard the seeds.

3 Prepare the brioche dough, and roll out on a floured surface into an 8-by-4-inch (20-by-10-cm) rectangle. Lay the grilled eggplants in the center of the dough, leaving a border of about 3 inches (7.5cm)

around the edges.

4 Place the peeled peppers on top of the eggplants and season with salt and pepper.

5 Put the sliced mozzarella in the center, being careful not to spread it out too far, so that the mozzarella is surrounded by the eggplants and peppers.

6 Then roll up tightly into an oblong sausage shape. Preheat the oven to 425°F (220°C).

7 Lightly coat the brioche with the egg and bake for 20–25 minutes, or until golden.

8 To serve, dress the salad leaves with the dressing. Cut a slice from the hot roll and garnish with the salad.

BRIOCHE

1lb (500g) brioche dough:
see recipe on page 154

Crescenta of Mozzarella & Roasted Peppers with Anchoiade

INGREDIENTS

Serves 4–6

Crescenta

METHOD

1 In a bowl, combine the flour, salt, baking soda, and milk. Stir, then knead to form a smooth dough, being careful not to overwork it.

2 Wrap the dough in a kitchen towel and leave for 1 hour.

3 Break off golf-ball-sized pieces of dough and roll out on a floured surface into very thin disks 7 inches (18cm) in diameter.

4 Fry the disks one at a time in plenty of olive oil, shaking the pan vigorously until the crescenta aeirate and become crisp and golden.

5 Drain on paper towels, then sprinkle with sea salt and keep warm until ready to serve.

CRESCENTA

1²⁄₃ cups (8oz/250g) "0" Italian flour or all purpose (plain) flour

pinch of salt

pinch of baking soda (bicarbonate of soda)

½ cup (4floz/125ml) milk

extra-virgin olive oil for frying

sea salt

Dressing

METHOD

1 Heat a little olive oil in a small pan. Add the shallot and garlic and cook gently until soft.

2 Add the anchovy fillets, white wine and basil leaves, and bring to a boil.

3 Now combine the anchovy mixture, mayonnaise, warm water and extra-virgin olive oil in a food processor and blend until smooth.

4 Pass through a fine-mesh sieve and season with salt and pepper.

DRESSING

olive oil for cooking

½ tin of good anchovy fillets in oil

⅓ cup (2oz/60g) finely chopped shallot

2½ tbsp finely chopped garlic

3 cups (3oz/90g) basil leaves

²⁄₃ cup (5floz/160ml) white wine

1 tbsp mayonnaise

1 tbsp warm water

2 tbsp extra-virgin olive oil

salt & ground pepper

Recipe continued on next page …

TOPPING

olive oil for roasting

2 large red bell peppers
  (capsicums)

sea salt

14 oz (400g) arugula
  (rocket) leaves

3 oz (90g) shallots, thinly
  sliced into rings

½ cup (4 fl oz/125ml)
  extra-virgin olive oil

4 balls (4 oz/125g each)
  buffalo mozzarella

12 anchovy fillets in oil

... continued from previous page

Topping

METHOD

1 *Preheat an oven to 500°F (260°C). Heat a baking sheet (tray) in the oven until very hot, add a little olive oil, and heat the oil.*

2 *When the oil is smoking add the peppers and roast, turning, until blistered all over, about 2 minutes. Sprinkle with sea salt.*

3 *Remove from the heat, place in a bowl and cover with plastic wrap (cling film).*

4 *Once cool, remove the plastic wrap and peel and seed peppers carefully.*

5 *Cut into 12 large strips and sear on the stove top in a hot, almost dry pan.*

Assembly

1 *Toss together arugula leaves and shallots in a little of the extra-virgin olive oil.*

2 *Cut each ball of mozzarella into 3 thick segments.*

3 *Arrange mozzarella on the crescenta, then arrange anchovy fillets and roasted pepper strips on the bread.*

4 *Scatter the arugula and shallots on top and a little sea salt.*

5 *Then spoon the anchovy sauce around and over the crescenta, and finish with a light drizzle of extra-virgin olive oil.*

Baked Shallot & Oven-Dried Tomato Focaccia with Bocconcini

METHOD

1 *A day in advance, slice tomatoes in half and lay cut side up on tray. Sprinkle with olive oil, sea salt and pepper. Place in oven on lowest heat to dry overnight.*

2 *To make the focaccia, in a small bowl, sprinkle the yeast over the warm water and let stand until foamy, about 5 minutes. Mix the flour, a pinch of salt and the olive oil in a large bowl and add the yeast mixture. Mix and then knead until a soft, smooth dough forms. Place in bowl, cover and leave in a warm place to rise for an hour.*

3 *Preheat an oven to 400°F (200°C). Heat the whole shallots gently in a small pan with a little olive oil and the chopped herbs, then roast in the oven until tender, about 15 minutes. Allow to cool in the oil. Brush a baking sheet (tray) with olive oil. Leave the oven on.*

4 *Cut the dough into 4 equal parts and shape into balls, dusting with a little extra flour if necessary. Roll into flat ovals approximately ½ inch (12 mm) thick and lay them on the baking sheet.*

5 *Push the shallots into the dough decoratively and drizzle with a little of the shallot oil. Bake for 10 minutes. Add the dried tomatoes to the top and bake again for 4–5 minutes, or until the focaccia is golden.*

6 *Place bocconcini on top, sprinkle with the whole thyme leaves and bake again for 2–3 minutes, or until the cheese just starts to melt.*

7 *Serve while still warm with a salad of mixed leaves tossed in olive oil.*

INGREDIENTS

serves 6

1 lb (500g) cherry tomatoes or very small tomatoes

olive oil

coarse sea salt

ground pepper

12-18 shallots, peeled

1 tsp chopped thyme

1 tsp chopped rosemary

18 bocconcini

whole thyme leaves

FOCACCIA

1½ tsp active dry yeast

a little warm water

8 oz (200g) bread (plain strong) flour

pinch of salt

¼ cup (2floz/60ml) olive oil

Baked Shallot & Oven-Dried

Tomato Focaccia with Bocconcini

(recipe on previous page)

Rotolo of Wood-Roasted Eggplant & Peppers with Brioche

INGREDIENTS

serves 8–10

1 lb (500g) eggplant
   (aubergine)

olive oil

salt & ground pepper

1 lb (500g) red bell
   peppers (capsicum),
   peeled with a vegetable
   peeler

2 lb (1kg) brioche dough
   (see recipe page 154)

1 roll (2lb/1kg) buffalo
   mozzarella (rotolo),
   well drained

leaves from 2 bunches
   basil

1 egg, beaten

pesto (see recipe page 155)

METHOD

1 Cut the eggplant lengthwise into slices 1 inch (2.5cm) thick. Rub with olive oil and season with salt and pepper. Lay on a baking sheet (tray) and bake in a wood oven (or a very hot domestic oven) until browned.

2 Rub the peppers with olive oil and salt and bake as for the eggplants, let cool and discard seeds.

3 Roll out the brioche dough on a floured surface into a rectangle about 20-by-15 inches (40-by-30cm) and ½ inch (12mm) thick, then place in refrigerator and leave.

4 Lay the drained mozzarella on a sheet of plastic wrap (cling film) and season, then lay the eggplant slices flat on top.

5 Cover the eggplant with the basil leaves, season with salt and pepper, then cover the basil with the roasted peppers.

6 Take care to mop up any excess liquid or juice that may run out.

7 Using the plastic wrap to help, roll the rotolo up like a jelly (Swiss) roll, making sure it is as tight as possible. Puncture a few holes in the wrap and leave in refrigerator to chill and drain for 1 hour.

8 Remove the brioche dough from the refrigerator, unwrap the rotolo and roll up in the brioche dough, then seal the ends.

9 Brush with egg wash and place on a baking sheet. Leave at room temperature for an hour to allow the brioche to rise, then bake in a preheated 325°F (170°C) oven for 25 minutes, or until golden.

10 Remove from the oven and leave for 5 minutes before serving. Cut a thick slice and serve with roasted eggplant and a spoonful of pesto.

Note: This dish can be served cold as a picnic item.

Focaccia with Buffalo Mozzarella & Rosemary

METHOD

1 Make the bread recipe outlined below.

2 Preheat a broiler (grill), or prepare a charcoal fire.

3 Broil (grill) or charcoal grill the dough rounds one at a time for about 2 minutes on each side until they bubble and brown.

4 Remove them to a cutting board and, while still hot, sprinkle with the mozzarella that has been passed through a food mill or coarse sieve. Lightly sprinkle with salt and pepper, a little rosemary and olive oil. Cut into wedges and devour.

INGREDIENTS

serves 6

2 balls (4oz/125g each) buffalo mozzarella

salt & ground pepper

rosemary leaves

extra-virgin olive oil

Focaccia

METHOD

1 Mix the warm water, yeast, sugar and half the flour in a stand mixer fitted with a dough hook for 10 minutes until sloppy and foaming.

2 Now add the remaining flour, salt and olive oil gradually.

3 Work the machine for a few minutes longer until a sloppy dough is collecting and twisting around the dough hook.

4 Generously oil a bowl. Flour your hands and transfer dough from mixer bowl to the oiled bowl. Slap the dough from side to side, flouring lightly until the oil is absorbed, then lightly oil the top of the dough, turn over and wrap in plastic wrap (cling film).

5 Allow to rise to double the size. Remove the plastic wrap and bash down the dough, repeating a few times, then leave for 10–15 minutes.

6 Roll out balls of the dough with your fingertips, to create several very thin rounds, each about 12 inches (30cm) in diameter.

7 Proceed with the rest of the recipe, as above.

FOCACCIA

4 cups (32floz/1liter) warm water

2 envelopes (2 tsps) active dry yeast

2 tsp sugar

9½ cups (3lb/1.5kg) "00" Italian flour or all-purpose (plain) flour

2 tsp salt

3 tbsp olive oil

Polenta, Mozzarella & Prosciutto Sandwich

serves 10–12

6 cups (48floz/1.5 liters)
  water

3 cups (24floz/700ml) milk

2 tbsp salt

3 cups (1lb/500g) polenta

²⁄₃ cup (5oz/155g) butter

1¼ cups (5oz/155g) grated
  Parmesan cheese

2 tsp white pepper

1 tbsp Dijon mustard

1¹⁄₃ lb (700g) buffalo
  mozzarella, sliced

8oz (250g) prosciutto,
  thinly sliced

all-purpose flour

2 eggs, beaten

2 cups (8oz/250g) fine
  dried bread crumbs

vegetable oil for deep-frying

grated Parmesean cheese
  for dusting

METHOD

1 *Bring water, milk and salt to a boil. Slowly whisk in the polenta and bring the mixture back to a boil, whisking constantly.*

2 *Turn the heat down and leave the polenta to bubble slowly for half an hour, whisking occasionally to prevent lumps from forming.*

3 *After about half an hour the polenta should be coming away from the sides of the pan. Remove from the heat and add the butter,*

Parmesan cheese and pepper and mix in well.

4 *Lightly oil a baking sheet (tray). Pour a thin layer of the polenta onto it and spread evenly. Allow to cool. Keep the rest warm.*

5 *When this layer has cooled, spread a thin layer of Dijon mustard over it and arrange the mozzarella to cover the whole area. Layer the prosciutto over the mozzarella.*

6 *Pour over the remaining warm polenta and spread*

it out thinly to cover the filling. Let cool for at least an hour.

7 *When cold, turn out the entire sheet in one piece and cut into small, neat triangles.*

8 *Coat each piece in flour, then the beaten egg and finally coat with bread crumbs. Deep-fry in hot oil until crisp and golden brown.*

9 *Serve with parsley salad and a dusting of Parmesan.*

Pasta

Simone Cerea / CARAVAGGIO
Fresh Linguine with Asparagus, Sun-Dried Tomatoes & Smoked Mozzarella

Chris Benians / DAPHNE'S
Spaghetti alla Sorrento

Antonello Tagliabue / BICE
Timballo of Eggplant & Orecchiette Pasta with a Mozzarella & Tomato Sauce

Stefan Cavallini / THE HALKIN
Ravioli alla Mozzarella

Theo Randall / RIVER CAFE
Rigatoni with Plum Tomato Sauce, Marjoram, Buffalo Mozzarella & Pecorino

Theo Randall / RIVER CAFE
Baked Buffalo Mozzarella on Pasta Frolla

Lorenzo Berni / SAN LORENZO
Le Penne dei Principi di Paternò

Fresh Linguine with Asparagus, Sun-Dried Tomatoes & Smoked Mozzarella

INGREDIENTS

serves 4

PASTA

1⅔ cups (8oz/250g) all-
    purpose (plain) flour

pinch of salt

1 egg

¼ cup (2floz/50ml) water

SAUCE

5oz (150g) asparagus,
    trimmed

3 tbsp unsalted butter

2 tbsp olive oil

8 sun-dried tomatoes

about ¾ cup (6floz/180ml)
    vegetable stock

3 tbsp grated Parmesan
    cheese

salt & freshly ground
    pepper

5oz (155g) smoked buffalo
    mozzarella, finely diced

METHOD

1 To make the pasta, place the flour and salt in a mixing bowl. Mix the egg and water together and fold into the flour until the mixture reaches an elastic and doughlike consistency. Cover and let stand for 2 hours. Break into 4 portions and roll out each into a thin sheet on a pasta machine or by hand. Cut into noodles about ⅛ inch (2mm) wide and sprinkle with flour to prevent them from sticking together.

2 For the sauce, cut the asparagus into cubes and boil for 2 minutes. Melt half the butter with half of the olive oil. Add the asparagus and sun-dried tomatoes and fry lightly. Add the stock and simmer for 5 minutes.

3 Drop the pasta into a pan of boiling salted water for 3–4 minutes, stirring occasionally. Drain off the water and add the asparagus mixture to the pan. Add the remaining butter and olive oil, the Parmesan, and salt and pepper. Gently mix together until it reaches a smooth and creamy consistency, then serve on 4 small heated plates, topped with finely diced mozzarella.

Spaghetti alla Sorrento

INGREDIENTS

serves 4

10oz (300g) spaghetti

8 ripe plum (Roma)
   tomatoes

2 balls (4oz/125g each)
   buffalo mozzarella

3 tbsp good-quality olive oil

coarse sea salt & ground
   pepper

leaves from ½ bunch basil

METHOD

1 *Drop the spaghetti into a large pan of boiling salted water to cook.*

2 *Meanwhile, cube the tomatoes and mozzarella and place in a bowl with the olive oil. Season with sea salt and pepper. Tear the basil leaves and scatter in.*

3 *When the spaghetti is al dente, drain and add to the bowl with the other ingredients, toss and serve.*

Note: This dish is so simple that all the ingredients must be of the highest quality. Since the "sauce" is raw, the end dish is purposely warm rather than hot and is intended for a light summer's lunch.

INGREDIENTS

serves 1

7 slices eggplant
   (aubergine)

salt

1 egg, beaten

½ cup (2oz/60g) fine
   dried bread crumbs

1¼ cups (10floz/300ml)
   preferred oil for frying

⅔ cup (2oz/60g)
   orecchiette pasta

¼ cup (2floz/60ml) fresh
   tomato sauce (see recipe
   page 155)

5 basil leaves

1oz (30g) buffalo
   mozzarella, diced except
   for 1 slice

1 tbsp grated Parmesan
   cheese

ground pepper

fresh tomato sauce and
   basil sprig for garnish

Timballo of Eggplant & Orecchiette Pasta with a Mozzarella & Tomato Sauce

METHOD

1 *Place the eggplant slices on a kitchen towel, sprinkle them with salt and let the water evaporate for about 10 minutes before drying them well.*

2 *Dip the slices in egg and then roll them in the bread crumbs. Fry them in the oil and then lay them on paper towels to absorb any excess oil. Line a small baking dish with some foil and then*

line with the eggplant slices, letting them overhang the edges. Preheat an oven to 350°F (180°).

3 *Cook the pasta al dente. Meanwhile, heat the tomato sauce and add the basil leaves. Drain the pasta and then sauté together with the tomato sauce. Then add the diced mozzarella (reserving a slice for decoration), the grated parmesan, and salt and pepper.*

4 *Transfer the pasta to the baking dish and cover the top completely with the eggplant overhang. Place in the preheated oven for 5 minutes, or until the mozzarella melts.*

5 *Turn the timballo out onto a plate, garnish with a spoonful of tomato sauce, a small basil sprig and a mozzarella slice.*

Ravioli alla Mozzarella

METHOD

1 Clean the artichokes in advance.

2 Heat a little of the olive oil in a heavy-bottomed saucepan, sauté the garlic and thyme, then add the artichokes and white wine and cover.

3 Simmer until the wine is reduced, then add the vegetable stock and cover again. When cooked, let them cool.

4 Remove the artichokes from the pan and dice. Cut the mozzarella into cubes. Place both ingredients in a bowl and add the basil, salt and pepper.

5 Cut the pasta sheets into forty 2-inch (5-cm) squares. On top of 20 squares place equal mounds of the artichoke-mozzarella mixture, then cover with the remaining 20 squares, pressing around the edges to make small parcels.

6 Cook the ravioli in a large pot of boiling salted water.

7 Meanwhile, chop the 4 tomatoes and sauté with the remaining olive oil. In a separate pan, melt the butter.

8 Drain the ravioli and arrange 5 ravioli on each plate. Top each with a few spoonfuls of the sautéed tomato. To serve, sprinkle with the pine nuts and Parmesan, and drizzle over the melted butter.

INGREDIENTS

serves 4

4 artichokes

2 tbsp extra-virgin olive oil

2 cloves garlic

1 thyme sprig

½ cup (4 floz/125ml) white wine

½ cup (4 floz/125ml) vegetable stock

3 balls (4oz/125g each) buffalo mozzarella

3 basil leaves, finely chopped

salt & ground pepper

4oz (125g) ravioli pasta sheets

4 tomatoes

¼ cup (2oz/60g) butter

2½ tbsp pine nuts

2 tbsp grated Parmesan cheese

Rigatoni with Plum Tomato Sauce, Marjoram, Buffalo Mozzarella & Pecorino

INGREDIENTS

serves 4

2 cloves garlic

¼ cup (2floz/60ml) extra-virgin olive oil

leaves from 1 bunch fresh marjoram

1 can (1lb/500g) plum (Roma) tomatoes, coarsely chopped

1lb (500g) rigatoni pasta

2 balls (4oz/125g each) buffalo mozzarella, cut into small pieces

1 cup (4oz/125g) grated pecorino or parmigiano-reggiano cheese

salt & ground pepper

METHOD

1 *Slice garlic very thinly and fry gently in olive oil until a light golden color.*
2 *Add marjoram leaves and cook for a few seconds. Reduce heat to low and add the tomatoes. Cook slowly for 40 minutes or until the mixture reaches a thick consistency.*
3 *Drop the rigatoni into a large pan of boiling salted water, and cook until al dente. Drain the pasta, add tomato sauce, fold in mozzarella, and pecorino, season with salt and pepper and serve.*

Baked Buffalo Mozzarella on Pasta Frolla

METHOD

1 Place all the pasta ingredients into a food processor and pulse until a dough forms. Wrap the dough in plastic wrap (cling film) and chill for a minimum of 45 minutes. This can be done 24 hours in advance.

2 Roll out the dough on a floured work surface into a 20-by-10-inch (50-by-25-cm) rectangle. Chill in refrigerator for a further 30 minutes. Remove dough from refrigerator, and cut into 6 equal squares. Bake on a baking sheet (tray) at 350°F (180°C) for 15 minutes, or until golden brown. Set aside to cool.

3 Preheat oven to 450°F (230°C). Cut each mozzarella ball into 4 slices and place on each square of pasta. Slice potatoes wafer-thin (if possible use mandoline or slicer on food processor; alternatively, blanch potatoes and slice as thinly as possible by hand).

4 Layer potato slices on top of mozzarella, with garlic, thyme, grated Parmesan, and generous amounts of pepper. Bake for 8–10 minutes, or until mozzarella begins to melt and Parmesan is golden.

5 If available, serve covered with thinly sliced white truffles. Otherwise, drizzle with good-quality truffle oil.

Note: White truffles are in season between mid-October and late December but are hard to come by, as well as expensive, and can probably only be used as an exceptional treat. Truffle oil is a good substitute.

INGREDIENTS

serves 6

PASTA FROLLA

½ cup (4oz/125g) unsalted butter

1⅔ cups (8oz/250g) all-purpose (plain) flour

¼ cup (2floz/60ml) ice water

pinch of salt

TOPPING

6 balls (4oz/125g each) buffalo mozzarella

4 waxy boiling potatoes, peeled

2 cloves garlic, thinly sliced

leaves from 4 thyme sprigs

1 cup (4oz/125g) grated Parmesan cheese

ground pepper

2oz (60g) white truffles (optional; see note)

Le Penne dei Principi di Paternò

INGREDIENTS

serves 4

6 tbsp (3floz/90ml) olive oil

1 onion, chopped

1 clove garlic, chopped

10oz (300g) tomatoes,
   peeled and chopped

salt & ground pepper

2 cloves garlic, whole

1 tsp tomato paste
   (optional)

2 tbsp coarse sea salt

1 lb (500g) penne pasta

8oz (250g) buffalo
   mozzarella

¾ cup (4oz/125g) black
   olives, pitted

a few basil leaves

METHOD

1 Begin by preparing a basic tomato sauce: Heat 3 tbsp of the olive oil in a frying pan and sauté the onion and the chopped garlic until golden.

2 Then add the tomatoes and season with salt and pepper. Add the 2 whole garlic cloves. Cook for about 20 minutes until the excess liquid evaporates, then remove the 2 whole garlic cloves. Add the tomato paste to enrich the taste, if desired.)

3 Bring a large pan of water to a boil, and add the coarse sea salt.

4 Add the penne to the boiling water and cook until al dente.

5 While the pasta is cooking, cut the mozzarella into small cubes.

6 When the pasta is ready, drain and place in a serving bowl, add the tomato sauce, the olives and mozzarella. Mix through gently. Drizzle over the remaining spoonfuls of olive oil, using more or less as preferred.

7 Serve immediately, garnishing the top with a few basil leaves.

Note: It is important that the mozzarella is added at the last moment when the pasta has cooled a fraction, to prevent the cheese from melting too much and becoming stringy.

Legumi

David Burke / LE PONT DE LA TOUR
Ballotine of Broiled Vegetables with Buffalo Mozzarella

Alberto Chiappa / MONTPELIANO
Mozzarella, Asparagus, Raisins & Pine Nuts with Vinaigrette al Peperone

Paul Wilson / GEORGES
Seared Tomatoes with Caponata & Mozzarella

Chris Benians, DAPHNE'S
Buffalo Mozzarella with Rolled Eggplant & Pesto

Chris Benians / DAPHNE'S
Buffalo Mozzarella with Peppers Piedmontese

Henrik Iversen / QUAGLINO'S
Buffalo Mozzarella with Couscous, Lemon, Parsley & Capers

Alastair Little / ALASTAIR LITTLE
Gâteau of Grilled Vegetables & Mozzarella

Matthew Harris / BIBENDUM
Fried Mozzarella with Anchovy Dressing, French Bean Salad & Parmesan

Stefan Cavallini / THE HALKIN
Fiori di Zucchina

Sally Clarke / CLARKE'S
Grilled Finger Eggplant with Purple Basil & Mozzarella

Alberico Penati / ANNABEL'S
Smoked Buffalo Mozzarella with Porcini

Simon Arkless / OXO TOWER
Baked Tomatoes with Basil Cream & Melted Mozzarella on Herb Crostini

Henrik Iversen / QUAGLINO'S
Eggplant & Buffalo Mozzarella Beignet with Salsify & Balsamic

Alberico Penati / HARRY'S BAR
Sculpted Vegetables with Bocconcini

Alberico Penati / HARRY'S BAR
Bean Pâté & Buffalo Mozzarella with Vegetable Mayonnaise

Simon Arkless / OXO TOWER
Broiled Flat Mushrooms with Melted Mozzarella & Sun-Dried Pepper & Pickled Chili Relish

David Burke / LE PONT DE LA TOUR
Buffalo Mozzarella, Tomato & Pesto Tart

Ballotine of Broiled Vegetables with Buffalo Mozzarella

METHOD

1 Roast the peppers in a 450°F (230°C) oven for 10 minutes until blistered. Remove from the oven and let them cool down. Peel off the skin, split in half and seed. Then broil (grill) on both sides for 2 minutes.

2 Slice the eggplants and zucchini very thinly, preferably on a mandoline. Season the slices with salt and pepper, brush with oil. Broil (grill) on both sides for 2 minutes. Let cool.

3 Lay a sheet of plastic wrap (cling film) on a flat surface, place the eggplant slices on top widthwise and brush lightly with some pesto.

4 Next place a layer of zucchini on top of the eggplants.

5 Using the plastic wrap as an aid, start to roll the layered vegetables as if making a jelly (Swiss) roll. Continue to roll very tightly until you have a cylindrical shape. Tie both ends of the ballotine tightly and refrigerate for 30 minutes.

6 Remove the plastic wrap and cut into 12 even slices. Divide equally among 4 plates with 3 slices of mozzarella on each. Finish with a little cracked pepper and some gazpacho if desired.

INGREDIENTS

serves 4

3 red bell peppers (capsicums)

3 eggplants (aubergines)

6 zucchini (courgettes)

salt & ground pepper

olive oil

½ cup (4oz/125g) pesto, (see recipe on page 155)

2 balls (4oz/125g each) buffalo mozzarella, cut into 12 slices

about 2 cups (16floz/500ml) gazpacho (optional)

INGREDIENTS

serves 4

⅓ cup (2oz/50g) golden
    raisins (sultanas)

12 asparagus spears,
    trimmed

1 clove garlic, unpeeled

2 tbsp olive oil

1 green (spring) onion

⅓ cup (2oz/60g) pine nuts

salt & ground pepper

4 balls (4oz/125g each)
    buffalo mozzarella

basil leaves

VINAIGRETTE

2 red bell peppers
    (capsicums)

2 shallots

1 clove garlic

4 tbsp olive oil

1 tsp balsamic vinegar

salt & ground pepper

1 tsp Dijon mustard

1 tsp tomato paste

Mozzarella, Asparagus, Raisins & Pine Nuts with Vinaigrette al Peperone

METHOD

1 Soak the raisins in water for 15 minutes. Meanwhile, boil the asparagus in salted water for 2–3 minutes and then quickly cool the spears in cold water. Cut them in half lengthwise and then into 1 inch (2.5cm) pieces.

2 Gently fry the unpeeled garlic clove in oil. Coarsely chop the green onion, add to the garlic, and fry for another 2 minutes.

3 Remove the garlic and add the pine nuts, frying them slightly. Drain the raisins and pat dry on paper towels. Add to the green onions and pine nuts.

4 Add the asparagus, salt and pepper. Flash cook for 2 minutes, remove from heat and allow to cool.

5 For the vinaigrette, broil (grill) the peppers for 15–20 minutes until blistered. Remove and place on a dish; cover with plastic wrap (cling film) for a few minutes so the skins come off easily.

6 Peel the peppers and remove the seeds. Coarsely chop the flesh and set aside. Fry the shallots and garlic clove for 2–3 minutes in 2 tbsp of the oil.

7 Remove the garlic, add the red peppers, salt and pepper, mustard and tomato paste. Cook slowly for 5 minutes and add 3 tbsp water.

8 Place in a blender and puree, then pass through a small sieve, whisking gently with a fork and adding the last 2 tbsp olive oil and the vinegar. Cut each mozzarella ball into 6 slices and place in a circle in a round dish so they overlap slightly. Place the asparagus in the center.

9 Garnish with the basil leaves and spoon over the vinaigrette.

Seared Tomatoes with Caponata & Mozzarella

INGREDIENTS

serves 6

6 cloves garlic

sea salt & ground pepper

juice of 1 lemon

about 3 tbsp extra-virgin
olive oil

3 tbsp balsamic vinegar

about 5 cups (5oz/155g)
loosely packed basil leaves

1lb (500g) plum (Roma)
tomatoes, peeled
(8 tomatoes)

1lb (500g) buffalo
mozzarella, thickly sliced

1 cup (1oz/30g) flat-leaf
parsley leaves

¼ cup (1oz/30g) shallot rings

Caponata

1 *Salt eggplants and allow to drain for 15 minutes.*

2 *In a large pan gently heat some of the olive oil and fry the celery with leaves and onions until soft, about 10 minutes.*

3 *Add garlic, eggplants, and remaining olive oil and stew gently for 30 minutes. Season with salt and pepper and add tomato puree. Cook gently.*

4 *Mix vinegar and sugar together in a separate pan, bring to a boil and taste. The mixture should have a pleasant sweet-and-sour taste; if not add more sugar or vinegar depending on your preference.*

5 *Add this to the eggplant mix and cook for a further hour until everything is well stewed like a compote.*

6 *Then add olives, capers and the basil, reserving a few capers for the final garnish. Check seasoning and allow to cool.*

Seared Tomatoes

1 *Crush garlic with a little salt and lemon.*

2 *Add most of the olive oil and mix in some of the vinegar.*

3 *Season with salt and pepper and add some of the basil, then set aside the marinade.*

4 *Heat a little of the olive oil in a very hot pan until oil is smoking.*

5 *Carefully add tomatoes, 2 or 3 at a time, and sear well on all sides.*

6 *Season while warm with salt and pepper and place in the marinade for at least an hour or more.*

7 *Place a generous spoonful of the room temperature caponata in the center of each plate; spread out evenly.*

8 *Place 2 seared tomatoes on the caponata. Place several slices of buffalo mozzarella next to the tomatoes. Season with salt and pepper.*

9 *Toss the remaining basil, the parsley and shallot rings in some of the remaining extra-virgin olive oil and arrange on top of the tomatoes and mozzarella.*

10 *Lastly, sprinkle on a few capers and drizzle over the remaining olive oil and balsamic vinegar.*

CAPONATA

salt

1 lb (500g) eggplants
(aubergines), cut into
1-inch (2.5-cm) dice

1¼ cups (10floz/300ml)
olive oil

1 lb (500g) celery with
leaves, cut into 1-inch
(2.5-cm) dice

1 lb (500g) onions, cut
into 1-inch (2.5-cm) dice

3 cloves garlic, chopped

ground pepper

¼ cup (2floz/60ml) tomato
puree

3 tbsp red wine vinegar

3 tbsp balsamic vinegar

⅓ cup (3oz/90g) sugar

1 lb (500g) green olives,
pitted

¼ cup (2oz/60g) capers

4 cups (4oz/125g) basil
leaves

Buffalo Mozzarella with Rolled Eggplant & Pesto

METHOD

1 *Prepare a charcoal fire. Thinly slice the eggplants lengthwise into strips so that you have at least 12 slices total. Lightly oil the slices and charcoal grill on both sides until cooked, then place on a platter, lightly brush with some of the balsamic vinegar and leave to cool.*

2 *Prepare the filling by mixing together the capers, tomato, olives, parsley and the remaining vinegar. Place a heaped teaspoon of filling on each slice of eggplant and roll it up.*

3 *To make the pesto, combine most of the basil, the pine nuts, garlic and the remaining olive oil in a mortar or a food processor*

and grind to a paste.

4 *Slice each ball of mozzarella into 6 pieces and place 3 pieces on each plate. Then place 3 of the eggplant rolls next to the cheese and spoon some of the pesto around. Garnish with the reserved basil leaves.*

INGREDIENTS

serves 4

2 eggplants (aubergines)

about 1 cup (8 floz/250ml)
  olive oil

1 tbsp balsamic vinegar

2 tbsp salted baby capers,
  rinsed

2 tbsp chopped tomato

1 tbsp chopped black olive

1 tbsp chopped parsley

2 cups (2oz/60g) basil
  leaves

3 tbsp pine nuts

3 cloves garlic

2 balls (4oz/125g each)
  buffalo mozzarella

Buffalo Mozzarella with Peppers Piedmontese

INGREDIENTS

serves 2

2 red bell peppers
   (capsicums)

2 yellow bell peppers
   (capsicums)

salt & ground pepper

4 garlic slices

4 basil leaves

8 salted anchovy fillets,
   rinsed (optional)

4 plum (Roma) tomatoes

1 tbsp olive oil

2 balls (4oz/125g each)
   buffalo mozzarella, sliced

basil leaves for garnish

METHOD

1 *Cut the peppers in half lengthwise through their cores, leaving them attached, and trim out the seeds. Season the insides of the peppers with salt, pepper, a slice of garlic, a whole basil leaf, and the anchovy fillets, if using.*

2 *Cut the tomatoes in half and place equal portions into the middle of each pepper. Then season again and drizzle with olive oil.*

3 *Place in an oiled, heavy-bottomed baking dish, cover with foil and bake in a pre-heated 350°F (180°C) oven for 1 hour.*

4 *After 1 hour, remove the foil and continue to cook the peppers for another 30 minutes. By this time the peppers should be very soft and the tomatoes slightly shriveled. Let cool, then serve with mozzarella slices and basil garnish.*

Buffalo Mozzarella with Couscous, Lemon, Parsley & Capers

METHOD

1 To make the couscous salad, mix the couscous with the cucumber, one-fourth of the olive oil, three-fourths of the tomato, half of the lemon juice, half of the chopped parsley, and three-fourths of the red onion. Season with salt and pepper.

2 Set aside the salad while you make the dressing, mixing together the remaining parsley, lemon juice and zest, diced tomato, capers, shallots, and olive oil. Season with salt and pepper.

3 Divide the couscous salad into 4 portions and press into a circular patty on each serving plate.

4 Arrange the mozzarella neatly on top.

5 Spoon some of the dressing over each plate, partially covering the mozzarella. Scatter on the Parmesan.

INGREDIENTS

serves 4

1²⁄₃ cups (10oz/300g) couscous, cooked

¼ cucumber, peeled and diced

1¼ cups (10floz/300ml) virgin olive oil

2 plum (Roma) tomatoes, peeled, seeded and diced

grated zest and juice of 1 lemon

1⅓ cups (2oz/60g) chopped parsley

½ red onion, diced

salt & ground pepper

2 tbsp capers

⅓ cup (1oz/30g) shallot rings

2 balls (4oz/125g each) buffalo mozzarella, sliced

1oz (30g) Parmesan cheese, shaved

Gâteau of Grilled Vegetables & Mozzarella

METHOD

1 *Preheat an oven to 325°F (170°C).*

2 *Scorch the peppers over a direct flame until blackened all over. Allow to cool a little, then peel quickly under running water over a colander. Pat dry, open out, remove seeds and cut the flesh into four 2-inch (5-cm) squares. Lay on a plate and season with salt, pepper and olive oil.*

3 *Cut the eggplants into 8 slices each ¹/₂ inch(12mm) thick. Season and oil gener-*

ously on both sides. Put on a baking sheet (tray) in a single layer and bake until collapsed and tender, 15–20 minutes. Remove from baking sheet and transfer to a large plate or baking sheet (tray).

4 *Peel the tomatoes and cut into 8 slices each ¹/₄ inch (6mm) thick, then lay them out on another large plate.*

5 *Cut the mozzarella into 8 slices. Leave in a sieve to drain.*

6 *Take 4 plates. Put 1 slice of eggplant on each plate.*

Lay a slice of mozzarella on top, then a slice of tomato and 1 basil leaf. Follow this with a piece of pepper, then mozzarella, then tomato and basil, and another eggplant slice to finish.

7 *Before serving, drizzle oil on top and scatter with torn basil leaves and chopped pitted olives, if using.*

Note: It is important that all the vegetables are correctly seasoned before assembly, and that the mozzarella is well drained.

INGREDIENTS

serves 4

1 red bell pepper
  (capsicum)

1 yellow bell pepper
  (capsicum)

salt & ground pepper

good-quality olive oil

2 eggplants (aubergines)

2 large ripe tomatoes

2 balls (4oz/125g each)
  buffalo mozzarella

16 basil leaves

handful of pitted olives
  (optional)

Fried Mozzarella with Anchovy Dressing, French Bean Salad & Parmesan

METHOD

1 To make the dressing blend the first 5 ingredients in a food processor until smooth. Then, with the motor running, add the oil in a thin stream (as if you were making mayonnaise). When finished, season with pepper. If the dressing seems too thick, add a little water to thin it until it reaches the consistency of heavy (double) cream. The dressing will keep in the refrigerator for 3 or 4 days.

2 Cook the beans in plenty of salted boiling water. When they are just cooked, take them out and run them under cold water until cool.

3 Now the mozzarella has to be coated with crumbs. To do this you need 3 bowls, 1 containing the flour, 1 with the beaten eggs and 1 with the bread crumbs. Cut each ball of mozzarella into 3 slices. Dip 1 slice of mozzarella at a time into the flour, making sure every inch is covered. Then dip into the egg, again making sure every bit is covered. Then dip into the bread crumbs. When all the mozzarella slices have been coated in bread crumbs, place them on a platter, making sure the pieces do not touch one another. They are now ready to cook when

you want.

4 When almost ready to serve, put the beans in a bowl and dress with the olive oil, shallots and salt and pepper. Divide the beans among 4 plates.

5 Heat the vegetable oil in a deep fryer, or deep frying pan, and fry the prepared mozzarella slices until golden. Do not crowd the pan. You can do a few pieces at a time and then keep them warm on a rack in the oven until they are all done.

6 Place 3 mozzarella slices on each mound of beans. Drizzle generously with the anchovy dressing, sprinkle with Parmesan and serve.

INGREDIENTS

serves 4

1lb (500g) haricot verts
   or other slender green
   beans, trimmed

2 cups (10oz/300g) all-
   purpose (plain) flour

2 eggs, beaten

2½ cups (10oz/300g) fine
   dried bread crumbs

4 balls (4oz/125g each)
   buffalo mozzarella

1 tbsp olive oil

3 shallots, finely chopped

salt & ground pepper

vegetable oil for deep-frying

¼ cup (1oz/30g) grated
   Parmesan cheese

ANCHOVY DRESSING

1 tin (2oz/60g) anchovy
   fillets in oil, drained

3 tsp capers

1 clove garlic

juice of 1 lemon

3 egg yolks

2 cups (500ml) olive oil

ground pepper

Fiori di Zucchina

INGREDIENTS

serves 4

8 large zucchini (courgette)
    flowers with squashes
    attached

8 oz (250g) buffalo mozzarella

1 tomato, finely chopped

2 anchovy fillets

2 basil leaves

salt & ground pepper

2⅓ cups (12oz/350g) all-
    purpose (plain) flour

1 pinch of baking soda
    (bicarbonate of soda)

⅔ cup (5floz/160ml) water

2 tbsp sweet-and-sour sauce

2 tbsp extra-virgin olive oil

2 cups (16floz/500ml)
    vegetable oil

METHOD

1 Remove the flowers from the zucchini and scoop out their fleshy insides. Slice the zucchini and put aside.

2 Cut the mozzarella into cubes and place in a mixing bowl. Add half of the chopped tomato. Chop the anchovies and basil and add these together with salt and pepper to season.

3 Gently open each of the flowers and fill with equal portions of the mozzarella mixture.

4 In a bowl, mix the flour with the baking soda. Add the water and whisk until a paste forms. Then set aside in the refrigerator.

5 In a shallow pan warm the sweet-and-sour sauce and add the rest of the tomato. This should stay on low heat to warm gradually while the next stages are prepared.

6 Heat the extra-virgin olive oil and sauté the sliced zucchini until tender. Drain and divide among 4 plates.

7 Now deep-fry the flowers, heating the vegetable oil to around 325°F (170°C). When lightly golden, remove from oil and drain on paper towels. Cut in half and place on top of the bed of zucchini. Spoon the heated sauce around the plate.

Grilled Finger Eggplant

with Purple Basil & Mozzarella

(recipe on following page)

Grilled Finger Eggplant
with Purple Basil & Mozzarella

INGREDIENTS

serves 6

6 small to medium Asian
   (slender) eggplants
   (aubergines)

8 tbsp (4floz/125ml)
   olive oil

coarse sea salt & ground
   black pepper

leaves from 2 bunches
   purple basil (or green if
   unavailable), chopped

12 balls (4oz/125g each)
   buffalo mozzarella

¾ cup (1½oz/45g) fresh
   bread crumbs, fried in a
   little olive oil until crisp
   and seasoned with salt &
   pepper

METHOD

1 Prepare a charcoal fire or preheat an oven to 400°F (200°C).

2 Slice eggplants in half lengthwise and drizzle half of the olive oil over the halves. If cooking over charcoal, cook until the bar marks are clearly defined on the eggplants, crisscrossing if desired. Season with sea salt and pepper and half the purple basil. If using an oven, place eggplant halves on a baking sheet (tray), season with salt, pepper and half of the chopped basil and roast in oven until almost tender, about 10 minutes.

3 Cut balls of mozzarella into halves, season with salt and pepper and arrange with eggplants on serving plates. Drizzle with the remaining olive oil.

4 To serve, mix the remaining basil with the toasted bread crumbs and sprinkle on top of the eggplants.

Smoked Buffalo Mozzarella with Porcini

INGREDIENTS

serves 4

10 oz (300g) red onions,
  cut into rings

½ cup (4floz/125ml) extra-
  virgin olive oil

8 small, porcini mushrooms

1 bay leaf

1 rosemary sprig

salt & ground pepper

4 thick slices smoked
  buffalo mozzarella, 4 oz
  (125g) each

¼ cup (2floz/60ml)
  balsamic vinegar

METHOD

1 *Brown the onions in half of the olive oil until they are just translucent.*

2 *Lightly cook the mushrooms with the bay leaf, and rosemary in the rest of the oil. Add salt and pepper.*

3 *In a hot nonstick pan, sear the mozzarella slices quickly on either side before they begin to melt.*

4 *On each of 4 serving plates, layer a base of red onions, a mozzarella slice, and the mushrooms and herbs. Sprinkle with the balsamic vinegar.*

Baked Tomatoes with Basil Cream & Melted Mozzarella on Herb Crostini

INGREDIENTS

serves 4

6 large, ripe plum (Roma)
tomatoes, cut in half
lengthwise and seeded.

olive oil

salt & ground pepper

1½ cups (12 floz/350ml)
heavy (double) cream

½ cup (4 floz/125ml) crème
fraîche

2 cloves garlic, crushed

1 small bunch basil, leaves
and stalks separated

1 tsp sugar

1 tbsp chopped mixed
herbs (tarragon, parsley,
chervil, basil)

4 slices country-style
bread, toasted and
rubbed with garlic and
olive oil

8 oz (250g) buffalo
mozzarella

2 tsp grated Parmesan
cheese

METHOD

1 *Place the tomatoes, cut sides up, in an ovenproof dish with a little olive oil. Season with salt and pepper and place in a preheated 375°F (190°C) oven for 10 minutes.*

2 *Meanwhile, put the cream, crème fraîche, garlic, basil stalks and sugar into a pan and simmer until reduced by a third. Roughly chop the basil leaves, add to the pan, and then pour this mixture over the tomatoes. Cook in the oven for a further 15 minutes. The cream should have thickened and taken on a slightly pink hue from the tomatoes.*

3 *Meanwhile, sprinkle the chopped herbs on top of the toasted bread and slice the mozzarella.*

4 *When the tomatoes are cooked, remove them from the cream, place 3 halves on each piece of toast, sprinkle with a little parmesan and finish with a slice of mozzarella.*

5 *Place on a baking sheet (tray) and cook for a further 5 minutes, or until the cheese begins to melt. Remove from the oven and place on a warm plate. Pour the reduced basil cream around and complete with a generous twist of black pepper.*

Eggplant & Buffalo Mozzarella Beignet with Salsify & Balsamic

INGREDIENTS

serves 4

16 cherry tomatoes

rock salt

1 cup (8floz/250ml) dark beer

2 eggs, beaten

2½ cups (10oz/300g) all-
purpose (plain) flour

1½ oz (45g) Parmesan cheese,
shaved

salt & ground pepper

2 medium eggplants
(aubergines)

½ cup (4floz/125ml) pesto
(see recipe page 155)

3 balls (5oz/150g each)
buffalo mozzarella, halved

oil for deep-frying

2 sticks salsify (oyster plant),
scrubbed

extra-virgin olive oil

balsamic vinegar (12-year-old)

16 basil leaves

METHOD

1 In advance, pierce the cherry tomatoes and lay on a baking sheet (tray) on a bed of rock salt. Roast at 250°F (120°C) for an hour.

2 Meanwhile, prepare the batter by mixing together the beer, eggs, and half the flour. Whisk together, then strain through a sieve and season with salt and pepper.

3 Cut the eggplants into 12 even slices, season each with salt and pepper and spread with some of the pesto.

4 Place half a mozzarella ball on each of 6 slices, then top with another slice of eggplant, pesto side down to make a sandwich. Mix the remaining pesto into the beer batter.

5 Coat each sandwich evenly in remaining flour, shaking off any excess, then dip into the batter. Pour oil to a depth of 4 inches (10cm) in a deep fryer or saucepan and heat to 300°F (150°C). In batches, fry the coated sandwiches until golden brown, then remove, drain on paper towel, and season.

6 Cut the salsify in fine long ribbons. In a warm saucepan heat a little olive oil, then add the salsify, season, and cook for 2–3 minutes. Add a little balsamic, the basil and tomatoes. Remove from heat and use immediately.

7 To serve, cut each beignet in half and place 3 halves, cut side down on each of 4 plates. Arrange the salsify, tomato and basil neatly on each plate, then spoon over the remaining balsamic and some olive oil.

Sculpted Vegetables with Bocconcini

METHOD

1 *Trim the zucchini and daikons, and cook each separately in salted water. Boil the turnips in salted water, adding the saffron toward the end for just a few seconds to color the turnips lightly.*

2 *Cut the tomatoes into cylinders, and sculpt the cooked vegetables, including the beets, into shapes as desired.*

3 *For the dressing, mix the olive oil and lemon juice with the cloves and nutmeg and coriander to taste.*

4 *Arrange the vegetables and mozzarella on 4 serving plates and drizzle over the dressing.*

INGREDIENTS

serves 4

4 baby zucchini (courgettes)

4 daikons (Japanese radishes)

4 turnips

few saffron threads

4 tomatoes

2 large beets (beetroots), cooked

½ cup (4 fl oz / 125 ml) extra-virgin olive oil

juice of 1 lemon

5 cloves

ground nutmeg

ground coriander

16 mozzarella bocconcini

Bean Pâté with Buffalo Mozzarella & Vegetable Mayonnaise

INGREDIENTS

serves 4

4 cups (28oz/875g) drained
  cooked cannellini beans

¼ cup (2oz/60g) ricotta
  cheese

6 tbsp (3floz/90ml) olive oil

salt & ground pepper

finely chopped herbs

8oz (250g) buffalo
  mozzarella treccine,
  cut into 4 pieces (or 4
  mozzarella balls if
  unavailable)

herbs for garnish

VEGETABLE
MAYONNAISE

8oz (250g) vegetables
  (green beans, spinach
  and zucchini/courgettes),
  steamed

⅔ cup (5floz/150ml) extra-
  virgin olive oil

METHOD

*1 To make the pâté,
place half of the cooked
beans and all of the ricotta
cheese into a food processor.
Blend on maximum speed
for 20 seconds, and then
press through a sieve. Whip
the mixture together with
4 tbsp (2floz/60ml) of the
olive oil. Season with salt
and pepper.*

*2 To make the vegetable
mayonnaise, blend the vegetables and oil on maximum
speed for 20 seconds.*

*3 To serve, arrange the pâté
attractively at the bottom of
each plate. Arrange the rest
of the beans on the other
side of the plate and dress
with the herbs and the
remaining oil. Arrange the
mozzarella on top of this
with a pinch of salt and
spoon over the mayonnaise.
Decorate with fresh herbs.*

Broiled Flat Mushrooms & Melted Mozzarella with Sun-Dried Pepper & Pickled Chili Relish

INGREDIENTS

serves 4

3½ oz (100g) sun-dried
  peppers (see note)

2oz (60g) Spanish pickled
  chilies

1 clove garlic, crushed

¼ cup (1½oz/45g) pine
  nuts, lightly toasted

1 small bunch basil, finely
  chopped

2 tbsp of good-quality
  balsamic vinegar

¼ cup (2floz/60ml) extra-
  virgin olive oil

salt & ground pepper

4 very large, flat
  mushrooms each about
  5 inches (13cm) in
  diameter

8oz (250g) buffalo
  mozzarella

2 tbsp grated Parmesan
  cheese

METHOD

1 Prepare the relish in advance. Thinly slice the sun-dried peppers and then cover with a little boiling water to reconstitute for about 20 minutes. Pour off excess water. Thinly slice the pickled chilies, discarding the stalks. (Pickled chilies come in varying degrees of strength; if the chilies are too hot for you, discard the seeds from the middle before slicing).

2 In a bowl, mix the peppers, chilies, garlic, pine nuts, basil, balsamic vinegar and some of the olive oil. Season with salt and pepper and the relish is ready.

3 Next, lightly peel the mushroom caps and remove the stems. Brush with the remaining olive oil, season and cook under a hot broiler or in a 450°F (230°C) oven on a baking sheet (tray) for 6–8 minutes, or until tender.

4 Cut the mozzarella slices ½ inch (12mm) thick and spread on top of the mushrooms. Season the mozzarella and sprinkle the Parmesan on top. Return to the broiler or oven until the cheese melts and is a light golden brown on top.

5 Transfer to a warmed plate. Spoon the relish around and serve immediately.

Note: Sun-Dried peppers may be hard to obtain; if so fresh red peppers can be used. Just seed, thinly slice and sauté in a frying pan with olive oil and salt and pepper until the peppers are soft.

Buffalo Mozzarella, Tomato & Pesto Tart

METHOD

1 *Preheat an oven to 375°F (190°C).*

2 *Roll out the pastry ⅛ inch (3mm) thick.*

3 *Using a round pastry cutter, cut out 4 disks each about 5 inches (13 cm) in diameter. Prick the center of each disk with a fork.*

4 *On each pastry disk place alternate slices of mozzarella and tomato, then top with pesto, dividing it evenly. Refrigerate for 15 minutes.*

5 *Remove from the refrigerator and brush a little of the beaten egg on the edge of each disk. Place on a baking sheet (tray), lined with parchment (greaseproof) paper, and put in the oven. Cook for 15–20 minutes, or until the pastry is crisp and golden.*

6 *Remove from the oven and serve, drizzling a little of the basil-flavored olive oil on each tart.*

INGREDIENTS

serves 4

1 sheet puff pastry, 18 oz (560g), thawed if frozen

2 balls (4oz/125g each) buffalo mozzarella, sliced

4–6 large plum (Roma) tomatoes, blanched briefly and sliced

½ cup (4floz/125ml) pesto (see recipe page 155)

2 eggs, beaten

2 tbsp basil-flavored olive oil (or substitute shredded basil in olive oil)

Riso e Risotto

Simon Arkless / OXO TOWER
Butternut Squash, Mozzarella & Caramelized Garlic Risotto with Crispy Shallots & Pesto

Alberto Chiappa / MONTPELIANO
Risotto Mantecato

Henry Harris / FIFTH FLOOR, HARVEY NICHOLS
Spiced Tomato & Mozzarella Risotto

Matthew Harris / BIBENDUM
Saffron & Mozzarella Risotto with Arugula

Alberico Penati / ANNABEL'S
Red Onions & Buffalo Mozzarella on a Bed of Wild Rice

Dean Carr / THE AVENUE
Mozzarella, Basil & Tomato Risotto

Theo Randall / RIVER CAFE
Risotto with Pancetta Affumicata, Buffalo Mozzarella & Savoy Cabbage

Butternut Squash, Mozzarella & Caramelized Garlic Risotto with Crispy Shallots & Pesto

METHOD

1 *First make the pesto. Put basil, garlic, and pine nuts in a food processor with a little salt and pepper. Work to a paste, then add enough olive oil to produce a loose-textured puree. Remove from the food processor, pour into a bowl and fold in the Parmesan.*

2 *Next, dust the shallots in seasoned flour, shaking off any excess. Heat vegetable oil to 300°F (150°C) in a deep pan and deep-fry the shallots until lightly golden. Drain on paper towels, season with a little salt and keep ready on a warmed plate.*

3 *To caramelize the garlic, first blanch the garlic in a pan of salted boiling water for about 3 minutes, drain, transfer to a clean pan and add 1 cup (8floz/250ml) of the chicken and a knob of the butter. Cook until the garlic is soft and the stock is reduced down to a syrup that will coat the garlic cloves.*

4 *Peel and seed the butternut squash, cut into ½ inch (12mm) cubes and fry in a little olive oil until lightly colored. Transfer to a preheated 350°F (180°C) oven for 10–12 minutes, or until the flesh is tender. Meanwhile, gently sweat the onion in the remaining butter until the onion is soft but not colored.*

5 *Add the rice to the onions, raise the heat and toast until the rice is shiny and opaque. Lower the heat and begin to add the stock, a ladleful at a time. Stir into the rice and wait for it to become completely absorbed before you add the next one.*

6 *Once the rice is cooked (al dente) and of the correct texture, fold in the mozzarella, Parmesan and butternut squash and cook for 2 minutes more. Serve immediately on a hot plate, drizzle the pesto around the risotto and top off with a small pile of crisp shallots.*

INGREDIENTS

serves 4

2oz (60g) shallots, thinly sliced

¾ cup (4oz/125g) seasoned all-purpose (plain) flour

vegetable oil for frying

salt

16 cloves garlic, peeled

6½ cups (52floz/1.6liters) chicken stock, hot

6 tbsp (3oz/90g) unsalted butter

1 butternut squash, (1lb/500g)

olive oil

1 small onion, finely chopped

2 cups (14oz/400g) Arborio rice

4oz (125g) buffalo mozzarella, cut into ½ inch (12mm) cubes

½ cup (2oz/60g) grated Parmesan cheese

PESTO

leaves from 1 large bunch basil

3 cloves garlic

3 tbsp pine nuts, lightly toasted

salt & ground pepper

olive oil

3 tbsp grated Parmesan cheese

Risotto Mantecato

INGREDIENTS

serves 4

1 shallot

2 tbsp olive oil

1¾ cups (12 oz/375 g)
Arborio rice

4½ cups (36 floz/1 liter)
chicken stock, hot

5 oz (155 g) smoked buffalo
mozzarella, finely diced

½ cup (2 oz/60 g) grated
Parmesan cheese

½ cup (4 oz/125 g) butter

salt & ground pepper

½ cup (4 floz/125 ml) good
meat stock (optional;
see note)

METHOD

1 *Chop the shallot very finely and fry in the olive oil. Add the rice and cook for 2–3 minutes, mixing all the time.*

2 *Add half of the stock to the rice and cook for 15 minutes, adding the remainder of the stock a little at a time.*

3 *Remove from the heat and leave to cool for 2–3 minutes. Then start mixing vigorously with a wooden spoon while adding first the mozzarella, then the Parmesan, and then the butter.*

4 *Season with salt and pepper and serve.*

Note: If you want to use the meat stock as well, add half to the rice after the Parmesan, and pour the rest on top when serving.

Spiced Tomato & Mozzarella Risotto

(recipe on following page)

Spiced Tomato & Mozzarella Risotto

INGREDIENTS

serves 6

8 plum (Roma) tomatoes

4 cups (32floz/1liter)
   fresh chicken stock

½ cup (4oz/125g) butter

1 sweet white onion, finely
   chopped

1 tsp harissa (Moroccan
   hot suace)

grated zest of ½ lemon

1 clove garlic, finely
   chopped

2 cups (14oz/400g)
   Carnaroli or Arborino rice

3 tbsp grated Parmesan
   cheese

salt & pepper

12oz (350g) buffalo
   mozzarella

shaved Parmesan cheese

METHOD

1 *Preheat the broiler (grill). Broil (grill) the whole tomatoes for 5 minutes on each side or until the skin is blistered and the flesh is soft. Transfer to a blender and blitz to a puree. Push the puree through a sieve to remove the skins and seeds. Season and set aside.*

2 *In a medium saucepan, bring the stock to a boil and keep at a gentle simmer. In a wide stainless-steel pan, melt the butter and add the onion, harissa, lemon zest and garlic. Cook over gentle heat for 5 minutes. Add the rice and continue to cook for a further 2 minutes. Now add the fresh tomato puree and stir continuously until the rice has absorbed the puree.*

3 *Once the puree has been absorbed, add the hot stock a ladleful at a time, allowing the rice to absorb each dose of stock before the next one is added (this process should take 15–18 minutes).*

4 *Remove from the heat, stir in the grated Parmesan and check the seasoning. Finally cut the mozzarella into small cubes, return the pan to the heat and fold in the mozzarella. As soon as the mozzarella is heated through and has started to go stringy, it is ready to serve. Divide onto 6 plates and scatter over the shaved Parmesan.*

Saffron & Mozzarella Risotto with Arugula

METHOD

1 Gently fry the shallots in two-thirds of the butter for 4–5 minutes, or until they start to color, then add the rice and fry for a further 3 or 4 minutes, stirring so that all the rice is coated with butter.

2 Then add the saffron-infused chicken stock to the regular chicken stock. Bring this to a boil. Once the stock is boiling, the rest of the cooking process will take about 15 minutes.

3 Start adding the chicken stock to the rice bit by bit, stirring the whole time and only adding more stock when the rice has absorbed the previous ladleful. Continue with this until the rice is al dente and the stock is absorbed.

4 Season with salt and pepper and stir in the remaining butter. You are now ready to serve, but just before you do, stir in the mozzarella. This only needs to go in 1 minute before you serve, so it is just melting.

5 In another pan wilt the arugula in a bit of olive oil. Then serve the risotto in a bowl with a spoonful of wilted arugula on top and sprinkle with Parmesan.

INGREDIENTS

serves 6

4 oz (125g) shallots, finely chopped

¾ cup (6oz/185g) butter

1½ cups (10oz/310g) Arborio rice

1 tsp saffron threads infused in 2 tbsp chicken stock

4½ cups (36floz/1 liter) chicken stock

salt & ground pepper

3 balls (4oz/125g each) buffalo mozzarella, cut into ½-inch (12-mm) cubes

6 handfuls arugula (rocket) leaves

olive oil

3 tbsp grated Parmesan cheese

Saffron & Mozzarella Risotto with

Arugula (recipe on preceding page)

Red Onions &
Buffalo Mozzarella
on a Bed of Wild Rice

INGREDIENTS

serves 4

5oz (155g) red onions

1 lb (500g) buffalo mozzarella

about 1 cup (4oz/125g)
   shelled fava (broad) beans

¾ cup (5oz/150g) wild rice,
   cooked in salted water
   for 15 minutes and drained

BASIL DRESSING

½ cup (4floz/125ml) olive oil

1 tbsp lemon juice

salt & ground pepper

2 cups (2oz/60g) basil leaves

METHOD

1 *To make the dressing, combine all the ingredients in a blender and puree.*

2 *Cut the onions thinly into rings and dress lightly.*

3 *Cut the mozzarella into 4 thick slices and dress.*

4 *Cook the fava beans in salted water until tender, drain, peel off thin skin from each bean, cool, then dress.*

5 *On each plate, arrange a patty of cold rice. Place the mozzarella and onions on top. Arrange the fava beans and the rest of the dressing around this.*

Mozzarella, Basil & Tomato Risotto

METHOD

1 In advance, thinly slice one of the plum tomatoes (unskinned), sprinkle with a little salt and leave on a wire tray overnight to dry.

2 Plunge the remaining plum tomatoes in a small pan of boiling water for 10 seconds. Remove the tomatoes and put them into ice water. When they are cold, peel and quarter, remove seeds and dice into 1¼-inch (3-cm) chunks.

3 Melt half the butter in a heavy-bottomed pan. Add the shallots, garlic and rice and cook for 3–4 minutes to coat the rice..

4 Add half the vegetable stock to the pan, stirring constantly to stop the rice from sticking. Gradually add the remaining stock. The rice is ready when almost all the stock has been absorbed and the grains are al dente.

5 Remove from the heat, add the cream, mozzarella, diced plum tomatoes, remaining butter, and most of the basil, leaving a little for garnishing.

6 On serving, garnish with the remaining basil and the dried sliced tomato.

INGREDIENTS

serves 6

5 plum (Roma) tomatoes

salt

¼ cup (2oz/60g) unsalted
  butter

2 shallots, chopped

1 clove garlic, chopped

1½ cups (10oz/310g)
  Arborio or other
  risotto rice

4½ cups (36floz/1liter)
  vegetable stock, hot

1 cup (8floz/250ml) heavy
  (double) cream

4oz (125g) buffalo
  mozzarella, diced

leaves from 1 small bunch
  basil

Risotto with Pancetta Affumicata, Buffalo Mozzarella & Savoy Cabbage

INGREDIENTS

serves 4

4 oz (125g) pancetta
affumicata (or substitute
uncooked pancetta)

1 clove garlic, sliced

½ head Savoy cabbage,
shredded into tiny pieces

salt & ground pepper

1 medium red onion

½ cup (4oz/125g) unsalted
butter

2 cups (14oz/440g)
Arborio rice

⅔ cup (5floz/150ml) dry
white wine

6 cups (48floz/1.5liters)
fresh chicken stock, hot

2 balls (4oz/125g each)
buffalo mozzarella, cut
into small pieces

1¼ cups (5oz/150g)
Parmigiano-Reggiano
cheese

METHOD

1 *Slice pancetta into matchsticks, and fry with sliced garlic until golden. Toss in the cabbage, place a lid on the pan and steam for about 5 minutes. Season with salt and pepper, remove from heat and set aside.*

2 *Chop red onion very finely. Heat heavy-bottomed saucepan and melt butter.*

When the butter starts to foam, add the chopped onion and cook over low heat for 2–3 minutes, or until soft but not brown.

3 *Add the rice, and stir continuously for about 3 minutes until the rice becomes opaque. Then pour in the white wine and allow to absorb. Start adding the simmering stock to the rice,*

ladle by ladle, stirring continuously. The rice is cooked when it has a thick, creamy consistency and an even, al dente bite to the grain.

4 *Incorporate the cooked pancetta and Savoy cabbage mixture. Fold in the mozzarella and Parmesan, season and serve.*

Pesce e Crostacei

Stefan Cavallini / THE HALKIN

Caponatina of Eggplant, Shrimp & Mozzarella

Simone Cerea / CARAVAGGIO

Buffalo Mozzarella with a Fan of Smoked Salmon & Belgian Endive

Henry Harris / FIFTH FLOOR, HARVEY NICHOLS

Treccine Dressed with Anchovies, Onion & Lemon

Alberico Penati / HARRY'S BAR

Bocconcini & Caviar

Alberico Penati / ANNABEL'S

Mozzarella & Crab Layers with a Saffron Sauce

Caponatina of Eggplant, Shrimp & Mozzarella

INGREDIENTS

serves 4

2 large eggplants
  (aubergines)

salt

3 tbsp olive oil

2 tbsp chopped onion

½ cup (2oz/60g) diced
  celery, blanched

⅓ cup (2oz/60g) olives,
  pitted and chopped

1 tbsp capers

2 tbsp pine nuts

2 tomatoes, chopped

2 balls (5oz/150g each)
  buffalo mozzarella, diced

20 large shrimp (prawns),
  peeled

1 tsp squid ink

juice of ½ lemon

METHOD

1 *Cut the eggplants into ½-inch (12-mm) cubes and cook them in a nonstick pan with a pinch of salt.*

2 *Sauté the onion in 1 tbsp of the olive oil, then add the celery, eggplant, olives, capers, pine nuts and tomatoes. When these ingredients have softened, add the mozzarella, at the last minute. Remove from heat and reserve.*

3 *Heat a little more of the olive oil and cook the shrimp. Meanwhile, mix the remainder of the oil with the squid ink and lemon juice.*

4 *To serve, arrange the Eggplant and mozzarella mixture in the center of each plate. Then arrange 5 shrimp per plate around the edge and drizzle with the squid ink dressing.*

Buffalo Mozzarella with a Fan of Smoked Salmon & Belgian Endive

METHOD

1 Panfry the endive leaves in a little olive oil until crispy and golden. Lay the leaves on the plate alternately with the smoked salmon in a fan shape.

2 Cut the mozzarella into thick slices. Sprinkle with basil, salt and pepper.

Place mozzarella slices at the base of each endive and salmon fan.

3 For the sauce, peel the red pepper carefully with a vegetable peeler and remove the seeds. Cut into 6 equal pieces. Place the shallot in a pan with 1 tbsp olive oil and the butter. Add the pepper

and fry gently for 10–15 minutes, or until softened.

4 Place the contents of the frying pan into a blender with the tarragon, basil, stock, and remaining oil. Blend until smooth and creamy. Season with salt and pepper, and use to decorate the plate.

INGREDIENTS

serves 4

leaves of 2 Belgian endive (chicory/witloof)

olive oil

5 oz (150g) sliced smoked salmon

8 oz (250g) buffalo mozzarella

finely chopped basil

salt & ground pepper

SAUCE

1 large red bell pepper (capsicum)

½ shallot, finely chopped

2 tbsp olive oil

knob of butter

2 tbsp tarragon leaves

leaves from ½ bunch basil

2 tbsp vegetable stock

salt & ground pepper

INGREDIENTS

serves 4–6

1 medium red onion

1 large lemon

12 good-quality salted
   anchovy fillets, rinsed

4 slices sourdough bread

1 tbsp olive oil

2 cloves garlic, peeled

4 buffalo mozzarella
   treccine (or substitute
   mozzarella balls if
   unavailable

1 tsp thyme leaves

2 tbsp coarsely chopped
   flat-leaf parsley

1 tbsp extra-virgin olive oil

ground pepper

Treccine Dressed with Anchovies, Onion & Lemon

METHOD

1 *Slice the onion as thinly as possible, then place in a bowl of ice water for at least 30 minutes.*

2 *Remove the rind and all pith from the lemon, segment it and then coarsely chop the flesh. Split the anchovy fillets lengthwise into thin strands and keep both to one side.*

3 *Preheat a ridged cast-iron stove-top grill pan. Brush the slices of bread with the olive oil and grill until nicely browned. While the bread is still hot, rub each slice on one side with the garlic cloves in order to flavor the bread. Then cut the bread into strips.*

4 *To serve, place 1 treccine on each plate, scatter over the anchovy, chopped lemon and thyme. Remove the onion from the ice water, shake it dry and arrange a tangle of it on each cheese. Scatter the grilled bread and chopped parsley around the edge, and finish it off with a good drizzle of the extra-virgin oil and generous milling of black pepper.*

Bocconcini & Caviar

METHOD

1 *Prepare the puree in a blender, then add 1 tbsp of the olive oil, season with salt and pepper and stir to a smooth consistency.*
2 *Place equal portions of caviar on each plate, shaping into a circular patty. Shape the puree into* mounds and place 3 around each caviar patty.
3 *Garnish each mound with the tomato, chives and a little of the remaining olive oil. Place a bocconcino on top of each caviar patty and drizzle with the remaining olive oil.*

INGREDIENTS

Serves 4

²/₃ cup (5oz/150g) puree made with half watercress and half boiled spinach

4 tbsp (2floz/60ml) olive oil

salt & ground pepper

5oz (155g) Osetra caviar

1 tomato, cut into 2-inch (5-cm) fingers

chives for garnishing

4 mozzarella bocconcini

Mozzarella & Crab Layers with a Saffron Sauce

INGREDIENTS

serves 4

6 balls (5oz/150g each)
    buffalo mozzarella

10oz (310g) crabmeat

3oz (90g) mirepoix of
    vegetables (green beans,
    carrots and asparagus)

2 or 3 saffron threads

butter

flat-leaf parsley for garnish

CITRONETTE

½ cup (4floz/125ml) olive
    oil

1½ tbsp lemon juice

salt & pepper

SAFFRON SAUCE

⅓ cup (3floz/90ml) heavy
    (double) cream

2 saffron threads

1 cup (8floz/250ml)
    mayonnaise

METHOD

1 *Cut the mozzarella into 12 even slices total.*

2 *Mix the citronette ingredients, and dress the crab.*

3 *Dice the vegetables for the mirepoix and blanch, adding saffron for a few seconds at the end. Drain, sauté the vegetables lightly in a little butter and mix with the crab.*

4 *For the sauce, bring the cream to a boil and add the saffron for a moment. Remove saffron, add the cream to the mayonnaise and mix well.*

5 *On each plate, arrange a slice of mozzarella, and on top of that a layer of crab. Keep alternating until you have 3 layers of mozzarella and 3 layers of crab. Spoon the sauce around it, and garnish with parsley.*

Carne

Henry Harris / FIFTH FLOOR, HARVEY NICHOLS
Burrata ai Tartufi Bianchi with Prosciutto & Deep-fried Artichokes

Paul Wilson / GEORGES
Warm Asparagus, Prosciutto & Mozzarella

Antonello Tagliabue / BICE
Veal Cutlet Stuffed with Mozzarella & Porcini

Simone Cerea / CARAVAGGIO
Veal Escalope with Fresh Spinach & Mozzarella

Quinto Cecchetti / LA FAMIGLIA
Veal Escalope with Eggplant & Melting Mozzarella

John Torode / MEZZO
Baked Mozzarella Wrapped in Prosciutto

Dean Carr / THE AVENUE
Bruschetta of Prosciutto & Mozzarella with Onion Marmalade

Sally Clarke / CLARKE'S
San Daniele Prosciutto with Buffalo Mozzarella, Figs & Balsamic Dressing

Burrata ai Tartufi Bianchi with Prosciutto & Deep-fried Artichokes

INGREDIENTS

serves 4

1 cup (8 fl oz/250 ml)

　Barbera d'Alba red wine

　or other good red wine

3 tbsp chopped shallot

1 tsp mascarpone cheese

½ cup (4 fl oz/125 ml)

　extra-virgin olive oil

8 cooked baby artichokes

　(bought from

　delicatessen)

1¼ cups (10 fl oz/300 ml)

　milk

2 cups (10 oz/300 g)

　seasoned all-purpose

　(plain) flour

oil for deep-frying

salt

2 Burrata ai Tartufi Bianchi

　(see note)

4 slices prosciutto

chopped chives

METHOD

1 Place the red wine and shallot in a small saucepan, bring to a boil and reduce by half. Remove from the heat and whisk in the mascarpone followed by the olive oil in a steady stream. Season and set aside.

2 Halve the artichokes, pass them through the milk and seasoned flour twice, and then deep-fry in oil until golden. Drain on paper towels and season with a little salt.

3 Place the Burrata in the center of a serving platter. Arrange the prosciutto and artichokes around the cheese. Finally drizzle over the dressing, sprinkle with the chives, and place the plate in the middle of the table with a serving spoon.

Note: Burrata ai Tartufi Bianchi is a mozzarella parcel stuffed with creamy shredded mozzarella and sometimes flavored with white truffle oil. It can be ordered from a specialist Italian grocer. If the Burrata is unavailable, substitute buffalo mozzarella drizzled with a little white truffle oil.

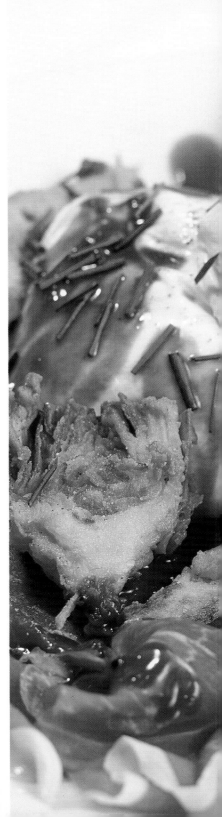

Warm Asparagus, Prosciutto & Mozzarella

METHOD

1 Peel asparagus spears 2 inches from the top, rinse, and cook in boiling salted water for roughly 4 minutes until tender, then refresh quickly in ice water. Keep warm until ready to serve.

2 Now take the mozzarella and slice each ball into 3 portions, season lightly with salt and pepper, and place a sage leaf on top of each slice of mozzarella.

3 Take each slice of prosciutto and slice lengthwise 3 times into thin strips. Place 1 slice of mozzarella at one end of each strip of prosciutto, and roll so that the prosciutto is wrapped around the center of the mozzarella.

4 In a hot pan quickly fry the asparagus spears in a little oil and a little of the butter until well-colored. Season and keep warm.

5 Now place a baking sheet (tray) under a hot broiler (grill) with a generous amount of olive oil.

6 When very hot, carefully place mozzarella slices on the baking sheet, turning over after 30 seconds. Remove from under heat once all of the mozzarella has been sealed.

7 Now gently heat up a small frying pan over medium heat. Meanwhile, arrange the warm asparagus on a plate, arrange the mozzarella slices on top and keep plates warm in a low oven.

8 In your warm frying pan, melt the remaining butter until it starts to bubble. Add the remaining sage leaves and continue to heat until they begin to brown. Add lemon juice, salt and pepper, then remove from the heat.

9 Remove plates of asparagus and mozzarella from the oven and generously spoon the sage butter all over and around the asparagus, then drizzle over a little balsamic vinegar.

INGREDIENTS

serves 4

20 asparagus spears, trimmed

4 balls (4oz/125g each) buffalo mozzarella

salt & ground pepper

2 cups (2oz/60g) sage leaves

4 thin slices prosciutto

olive oil

¾ cups (6oz/180g) unsalted butter

aged balsamic vinegar

3 tbsp lemon juice

Veal Cutlet Stuffed with Mozzarella & Porcini

INGREDIENTS

serves 4

4 veal cutlets (on the bone)

salt & ground pepper

5 oz (155g) of fresh porcini

mushrooms

1 cup (8fl oz/250ml) olive oil

1 clove garlic, chopped

2 tbsp chopped parsley

2 balls (4oz/125g each)

buffalo mozzarella

2 tomatoes, peeled and diced

¼ cup (1oz/30g) grated

Parmesan cheese

⅔ cup (5oz/150g) butter

1 small bunch rosemary

8oz (250g) mixed salad

leaves (curley endive

[chicory], radicchio

[red chicory], lettuce,

arugula [rocket])

24 basil leaves, chopped

METHOD

1 *Slice the veal cutlets in half lengthwise and flatten each half slightly. Season with salt and pepper.*

2 *Slice the mushrooms. Sauté half of the porcini in a little of the olive oil with the garlic and parsley.*

3 *Dice the mozzarella and place onto one-half of each cutlet, along with a few pieces of tomato, some Parmesan and the sautéed mushrooms. Place the other half of the veal cutlet on top, sealing the edges by pressing down with the back of a knife blade.*

4 *Brown the cutlets in a frying pan with all but 1 tbsp each of the oil and butter and the rosemary. Transfer to a baking dish and finish the cooking in a preheated 375°F (190°C) oven for 8–9 minutes, or until tender. Keep warm.*

5 *Place the remaining mushrooms into the frying pan with the veal juices still in it. Add the remaining 1 tbsp butter and cook until tender.*

6 *Sauté the salad leaves in a frying pan with the remaining 1 tbsp olive oil and arrange a bed of them on 4 serving plates. Place the veal in the middle and spoon over the porcini mushroom sauce. Garnish with the chopped basil.*

INGREDIENTS

serves 4

4 slices top veal round
   (rump), 5 oz (155g) each

olive oil

dash of dry white wine

5 oz (150g) spinach, boiled
   and drained

salt

2 tbsp grated Parmesan
   cheese

5 oz (155g) buffalo
   mozzarella cheese, cut
   into 8 slices

2 tomatoes, peeled and
   quartered

GARNISH

4 medium tomatoes

½ cup (1oz/30g) fresh
   bread crumbs

1 tbsp olive oil

2 tbsp finely chopped
   parsley

2 anchovy fillets, chopped

½ clove garlic, chopped

Veal Escalope with Fresh Spinach & Mozzarella

METHOD

1 Pound the veal slices to an even thickness. Fry in shallow, very hot oil until almost tender. Pour off the oil and add the wine, frying for a further 2 minutes. Take out the veal, reserving the pan juice for later.

2 Place the veal slices on a baking sheet (tray) and top with spinach, a pinch of salt, Parmesan cheese, 2 mozzarella slices and 2 tomato quarters.

3 For the garnish, slice the tops off the 4 tomatoes and seed. Mix the bread crumbs together with the olive oil, parsley, anchovies and garlic, and place inside the tomatoes. Place on baking sheet with veal and cook in a preheated 400°F (200°C) oven for 6–8 minutes, or until the cheese is golden brown.

4 Serve 1 slice of veal and 1 tomato on each plate, surrounded with a little of the remaining stock.

Veal Escalope with Eggplant & Melting Mozzarella

INGREDIENTS

serves 4

4 veal escalopes

1¾ cups (9oz/280g) all-
    purpose (plain) flour

5 tbsp (2½floz/75ml) olive oil

dash of white wine

1 medium eggplant
    (aubergine)

2 balls (5oz/155g each)
    buffalo mozzarella, sliced

fresh tomato sauce (see
    recipe page 155), hot

basil leaves for garnish

METHOD

1 Coat veal escalopes with a light dusting of flour. Then fry on both sides in a little of the oil, adding the white wine. Set aside.

2 Slice eggplant lengthwise and fry in remaining olive oil until golden on both sides. Remove from pan.

3 Place a slice of eggplant on each piece of veal. Then arrange mozzarella slices on top. Put under a preheated broiler (grill) for a few minutes until the cheese has melted. Remove from broiler, spoon over the tomato sauce, and garnish with basil. Serve at once.

Baked Mozzarella Wrapped in Prosciutto

METHOD

1 For the sauce, heat 1 tbsp of the olive oil in a pan and sweat the shallot and garlic over low heat until soft.

2 Add the vinegar and cook for a further 3–4 minutes until reduced, then add the passata and tomatoes, and simmer for 3 minutes.

3 Add the herbs and remaining olive oil, and cook over very low heat for 10–15 minutes, stirring occasionally, until thick and

a deep red. Season with salt and pepper. Remove from heat, allow to cool, then push through a coarse sieve and set aside.

4 Preheat an oven to 300°F (150°C). Season the mozzarella with pepper and roll up in the prosciutto, allowing 2 slices per ball of cheese.

5 Heat the oil in a large frying pan over high heat until just smoking. Place the parcels in the pan and sear,

turning constantly, until the outsides are well colored, about 1 minute. Transfer the parcels to a baking dish and cook in the oven for 5–6 minutes.

6 Spoon tomato sauce in the center of individual plates and sprinkle with the chopped basil and tarragon. Set a mozzarella parcel on top, drizzle with olive oil and serve.

INGREDIENTS

serves 4

4 balls (4oz/125g each) buffalo mozzarella

ground pepper

8 thin slices prosciutto

1½ tbsp vegetable oil

TOMATO SAUCE

4 tbsp (2floz/60ml) extra-virgin olive oil

1 shallot, finely chopped

1 clove garlic, chopped

1 tbsp champagne vinegar

½ cup (4floz/125ml) passata (tomato puree)

6 plum (Roma) tomatoes, peeled and seeded

5 basil leaves

5 tarragon leaves

sea salt & ground pepper

TO SERVE

a little chopped basil and tarragon

olive oil to drizzle

Bruschetta of Prosciutto & Mozzarella with Onion Marmalade

INGREDIENTS

serves 4

3 white onions

¼ cup (2oz/60g) butter

1 clove garlic, chopped

pinch of thyme leaves

1 bay leaf

1 tbsp mustard seeds

¼ cup (2oz/60g) packed
   brown sugar

¼ cup (2floz/60ml) red wine

¼ cup (2floz/60ml) red
   wine vinegar

5oz (155g) buffalo mozzarella

1 medium focaccia or 4 slices
   good country-style bread

2 bunches arugula (rocket)

8oz (250g) sliced prosciutto

pepper

METHOD

1 *Cut the onions in half using a sharp knife. Remove the roots and slice thinly.*

2 *Melt the butter in a heavy-bottomed pan, and add the sliced onions, chopped garlic, thyme, bay leaf and mustard seeds. Stir continuously for 15–20 minutes over medium-high heat, allowing the onions to turn a golden brown.*

3 *Add the sugar, red wine and red wine vinegar and cover with parchment (greaseproof) paper. Reduce the heat to low and cook for 30–40 minutes to allow the marmalade to thicken.*

4 *Cut the mozzarella into 4 thick slices. Cut the focaccia into 4 equal squares and toast.*

5 *To assemble, spoon the onion marmalade onto a plate and place a piece of focaccia on top with arugula leaves. Arrange the sliced prosciutto and mozzarella on top. To finish, add a twist of black pepper.*

San Daniele Prosciutto with Mozzarella, Figs & Balsamic Dressing

INGREDIENTS

serves 6

2 tbsp pine nuts

6 ripe green or black figs

6 balls (5oz/150g each) buffalo
mozzarella, well drained

12 generous slices San Daniele
prosciutto or other good-
quality prosciutto

6 bread sticks

DRESSING

¼ cup (2 floz/60ml) extra-
virgin olive oil

1 tbsp balsamic vinegar

course sea salt & black pepper

METHOD

*1 Mix balsamic dressing
ingredients together, seasoning with salt and pepper.*

*2 Place pine nuts on a
baking sheet (tray) and bake
in a 350°F (180°C) oven
until golden. Allow to cool.*

*3 Wipe figs and trim tops
away. Cut into quarters
lengthwise.*

*4 Cut mozzarella as desired
and arrange neatly with
the slices of San Daniele
prosciutto and figs on
individual plates.*

*5 Sprinkle with pine nuts
and drizzle with dressing.
Serve with breadsticks.*

glossary

Aioli

Garlic mayonnaise ideally suited for use with fish soups, fish, egg and vegetable dishes.

Anchoiade

A paste of anchovies, garlic and olive oil, used as a spread or condiment.

Ballotine

A roll traditionally made from a poultry or game bird that has been boned and stuffed. It may be served hot with a sauce or served cold in aspic.

Beignet

A French-style fritter, usually of deep-fried choux pastry.

Brioche

Bread of a rich yeasty dough, using a higher proportion of eggs and butter than usual.

Ingredients (makes 1 loaf)
4 tbsp (2floz/60ml) milk, warmed
1 tbsp active dry yeast
4 cups (1¼ lb/625g) unbleached all-purpose (plain) flour, plus extra for dusting
2 tbsp superfine (caster) sugar
1 tbsp salt
4 eggs, beaten
1 egg yolk beaten with 1 tbsp milk for glazing
1⅓ cups (11oz/330g) unsalted butter, softened

Method
1. Place the milk in a small bowl and whisk in the yeast. Allow to stand for 5 minutes. Stir in 1 tbsp of the flour and the sugar and set aside for 30 minutes.
2. Place the remaining flour and salt and sugar in a mixing bowl and make a well in the center. Pour in the yeast mixture and the eggs. Using your fingers, lightly bring the flour and liquid together until a dough begins to form, then turn out on a floured board and knead for 15–20 minutes, or until elastic and smooth.
3. Gently beat the softened butter with the back of a spoon until smooth, then add gradually to the dough, about 2 tbsp at a time. Knead the dough between your fingertips to incorporate the but-ter until thoroughly combined. Repeat until all the butter has been added. Cover bowl with a clean towel and leave in a warm place for 2 hours, or until the dough has doubled in size. Knock back by either punching down or turning over on itself. Cover and let rest in the refrigerator for several hours, or preferably overnight, then use as directed.

Buffalo Mozzarella

A soft cheese made from buffalo milk, a specialty of Naples

Caponata

Italian-style ratatouille from Sicily, traditionally based around a mixture of onions, celery, toma-toes and eggplants (aubergines).

Carta Musica

A traditional Sardinian bread, also known as pane carasau, made without yeast and characterized by its crisp, paper-thin texture and golden color. It is cooked in large rounds on a baker's slab and keeps well over long periods. Carta musica refers to the thin parchment used classically for writing music. Crisp Armenean cracker bread (lahvosh) can be substituted.

Chanterelle

Mushroom variety native to France, featuring a small head and long stem. Also known as girolle.

Ciabatta

A long oval bread resembling the shape of a "ciabatta," a kind of homely slipper. The dough contains more water than required for most breads, and takes especially long to rise, creating a light bread with thin crust. Any good country-style bread can be substituted

Coulibiac

A classic Russian dish in which layers of fish, vegetables and eggs are wrapped in brioche pastry.

Focaccia

A thick, flat Italian bread made with flour, salt, yeast and water. It is often flavored with different ingredients such as olive oil, herbs, eggs or cheese.

Mayonnaise

A cold dressing made from egg

yolks. Mayonnaise ingredients should be kept at room temperature prior to mixing:

Ingredients
2 egg yolks
salt & ground pepper
1 tbsp lemon juice
1¼ cups(10floz/310ml) extra-virgin olive oil

Method
Prepare the mayonnaise in a mixer: Place the 2 egg yolks (these must be at room temperature) in the mixing bowl, add a pinch of salt, pepper, and half the lemon juice and start mixing at medium speed. Add the olive oil a few drops at a time, until it has all been absorbed into a thick mixture.

Orecchiette

A pasta originating in the Apulia region of Italy. The word translates as "little ears", referring to the small, husklike shape of the noodles.

Pesto

An Italian sauce particularly associated with the province of Liguria, renowned for its sweet basil and extra virgin olive oil.

Ingredients
2 cups (2oz/60g) basil leaves
3 tbsp pine nuts
3 cloves garlic,
2 tbsp grated Parmesan cheese
1 cup (8floz/250ml) olive oil
salt & ground pepper

Method
Puree the basil, pine nuts, garlic, cheese and a small quantity of the oil in a blender. With the blender on a slow setting, gradually add the rest of the oil. Season with salt and pepper. If making by hand, use a mortar and pestle to grind the basil, garlic and pine nuts to a paste, gradually adding the cheese until the paste is smooth. Then gradually stir in the olive oil. Store in a jar with a thin layer of olive oil on top.

Porcini

Wild mushrooms with thick bulbous stems; a specialty of Tuscany. Most commonly found in spring, between March and July, and in autumn from September to November. They are the best wild mushrooms for drying.

Rotolo

A roll of vegetables, cheese or meats wrapped in pasta or dough.

Salsify

A popular Mediterranean root vegetable with an oysterlike taste. Also known as oyster plant.

Timballo

Classic Italian dish usually made with a mixture of meat and vegetables cooked in a mold lined with pasta.

Tomato Sauce

A basic Italian-style recipe:

Ingredients
3 tbsp olive oil
1 onion, chopped
2 cloves garlic, chopped
1½ cups (8oz/250g) peeled and chopped tomatoes (fresh or canned)
salt and ground pepper

Method
Heat the oil in a frying pan and sauté onion with garlic until golden. Then add tomatoes, salt and pepper to taste and cook for about 20 minutes, or until the excess water evaporates. A tsp of tomato paste or puree may be added if desired.

Treccine

A plait of soft mozzarella cheese.

contributors

Simon Arkless

OXO TOWER

◆ *Butternut Squash, Mozzarella*
& Caramelized Garlic Risotto
with Crispy Shallots & Pesto
◆ *Broiled Flat Mushrooms & Melted Mozzarella*
with Sun-Dried Pepper & Pickled Chili Relish
◆ *Baked Tomatoes with Basil Cream*
& Melted Mozzarella on Herb Crostini

Lorenzo Berni

SAN LORENZO

◆ *Insalata del Principe di Napoli*
◆ *Le Penne dei Principi di Paternò*

David Burke

LE PONT DE LA TOUR

◆ *Panfried Ciabatta Sandwich*
with Buffalo Mozzarella
◆ *Ballotine of Broiled Vegetables*
with Buffalo Mozzarella
◆ *Buffalo Mozzarella, Tomato & Pesto Tart*

Chris Benians

DAPHNE'S

◆ *Spaghetti alla Sorrento*
◆ *Buffalo Mozzarella with*
Rolled Eggplant & Pesto
◆ *Buffalo Mozzarella with Peppers Piedmontese*

Dean Carr
THE AVENUE

- *Mozzarella, Basil & Tomato Risotto*
- *Broiled Vegetable & Mozzarella Salad with Roast Garlic*
- *Brioche with Peppers, Eggplants & Mozzarella*
- *Bruschetta of Prosciutto & Mozzarella with Onion Marmalade*

Stefano Cavallini
THE HALKIN

- *Ravioli alla Mozzarella*
- *Fiori di Zucchina*
- *Caponatina of Eggplant, Shrimp & Mozzarella*

Quinto Cecchetti
LA FAMIGLIA

- *Veal Escalope with Eggplant & Melting Mozzarella*

Simone Cerea
CARAVAGGIO

- *Buffalo Mozzarella with a Fan of Smoked Salmon & Belgian Endive*
- *Veal Escalope with Fresh Spinach & Mozzarella*
- *Fresh Linguine with Asparagus, Sun-Dried Tomatoes & Smoked Mozzarella*

Alberto Chiappa
MONTPELIANO

- *Insalata alla Sophia*
- *Mozzarella, Asparagus, Raisins & Pine Nuts with Vinaigrette al Peperone*
- *Risotto Mantecato*

Sally Clarke
CLARKE'S

- *Baked Shallot & Oven-Dried Tomato Focaccia with Bocconcini*
- *Grilled Finger Eggplant with Purple Basil & Mozzarella*
- *San Daniele Prosciutto with Buffalo Mozzarella, Figs & Balsamic Dressing*

Henry Harris
FIFTH FLOOR
HARVEY NICHOLS

- *Spiced Tomato & Mozzarella Risotto*
- *Treccine Dressed with Anchovies, Onion & Lemon*
- *Burrata al Tartufi Bianchi with Prosciutto & Deep-fried Artichokes*

Henrik Iversen
QUAGLINO'S

- *Warm Salad of Buffalo Mozzarella & Chanterelles with Cabernet Vinegar*
- *Buffalo Mozzarella with Couscous, Lemon, Parsley & Capers*
- *Eggplant & Buffalo Mozzarella Beignet with Salsify & Balsamic*

Michael Moore
BLUEBIRD

- *Flat Bread with Bocconcini, Spices & Anchovies*
- *Rotolo of Wood-Roasted Eggplant with Peppers & Brioche*
- *Polenta, Mozzarella & Prosciutto Sandwich*

Matthew Harris
BIBENDUM

- *Spiced Artichoke Salad*
- *Fried Mozzarella with Anchovy Dressing, French Bean Salad & Parmesan*
- *Saffron & Mozzarella Risotto with Arugula*

Alastair Little
ALASTAIR LITTLE

- *Focaccia with Buffalo Mozzarella & Rosemary*
- *Gâteau of Grilled Vegetables & Mozzarella*

Alberico Penati
HARRY'S BAR & ANNABEL'S

- *Chilled Tomato & Bocconcini Salad*
- *Smoked Buffalo Mozzarella with Porcini*
- *Sculpted Vegetables with Bocconcini*
- *Bean Pâté & Buffalo Mozzarella with Vegetable Mayonnaise*
- *Red Onions & Buffalo Mozzarella on a Bed of Wild Rice*
- *Bocconcini & Caviar*
- *Mozzarella & Crab Layers with a Saffron Sauce*

Theo Randall
RIVER CAFE

◆ *Rigatoni with Plum Tomato Sauce,*
Marjoram, Buffalo Mozzarella & Pecorino
◆ *Baked Buffalo Mozzarella on Pasta Frolla*
◆ *Risotto with Pancetta Affumicata, Buffalo*
Mozzarella & Savoy Cabbage

Antonello Tagliabue
BICE

◆ *Foccacia Toscana with Mozzarella,*
Roast Peppers & Basil Cream
◆ *Timballo of Eggplant & Orecchiette*
Pasta with a Mozzarella & Tomato Sauce
◆ *Veal Cutlet Stuffed with Mozzarella*
& Porcini

Paul Wilson
GEORGES (MELBOURNE)

◆ *Crescenta with Mozzarella, Roasted*
Peppers & Anchoiade
◆ *Seared Tomatoes with Caponata &*
Mozzarella
◆ *Warm Asparagus, Prosciutto &*
Mozzarella

Nino Sassu
ASSAGGI

◆ *Eggplant Salad with Carta Musica*

John Torode
MEZZO

◆ *Roast Tomato Salad with Sorrel &*
Artichoke Hearts
◆ *Brioche with Peppers, Eggplant*
& Mozzarella
◆ *Baked Mozzarella Wrapped in Prosciutto*

i n d e x

a c k n o w l e d g m e n t s

Francesco Moncada di Paternò thanks: Caseificio Flli. Fierro, in particular Giuseppe Fierro and Marco Fossataro; Dott. Nicola Damiani; Dott. Enzo Spagnoli; and Alan Parker from Central Scientific Laboratories. Kind thanks also to: Simon Hopkinson; La Picena, London; Kevin Gould; and Jario Chamorro-Rojas.

Sian Irvine would like to thank: Jake Curtis; Rebecca Wingrave; Steve Shipman; and Anna and Derek Irvine.

Buffalo Mozzarella supplied by Franceschiello/Blue U.K. Ltd. 8 Talina Centre, 23A Bagleys Lane, London SW6 2BW. T. 0171 610 6155. F. 0171 610 6133.

Additional photographs supplied by: The Hutchison Library
© Robert Aberman: p. 4, 6
Alessandro Melodia: p. 7, 9tr, 9bl, 10tl, 11